Where One Hears the Rain

Finding Your Voice and
Crafting Your Story,
from Inspiration to Publication

CHRIS EPTING

PERMUTED
PRESS

A PERMUTED PRESS BOOK
ISBN: 979-8-88845-461-9
ISBN (eBook): 979-8-88845-462-6

Where One Hears the Rain:
Finding Your Voice and Crafting Your Story, from Inspiration to Publication
© 2024 by Chris Epting
All Rights Reserved

Cover art by Jim Villaflores

PERMUTED
PRESS

Permuted Press
New York • Nashville
permutedpress.com

Published in the United States of America
1 2 3 4 5 6 7 8 9 10

For John Cheever

TABLE OF CONTENTS

FOREWORD

Writing a memoir is a deeply personal journey—a chance to reflect upon the twists and turns of one's life, the ups and downs, the triumphs and tribulations. It requires a skilled and empathetic collaborator who can unlock the memories and stories buried within and guide the author through the process of self-discovery. In Chris Epting, I found a gifted storyteller as well as an exceptional collaborator who made the experience of writing my memoir, *Change of Seasons*, truly rewarding.

When I began the process of sharing my life story, I knew I needed someone who could help me capture the essence of my experiences and translate them into words that would resonate with readers. Chris proved to be the perfect partner in this endeavor. His diligence and passion for storytelling were evident from our very first meeting. He immersed himself in my world, meticulously researching and delving into the details that shaped my life and career.

What struck me most about Chris was his ability to listen and to truly *hear*. He possessed a unique talent for drawing out the nuances and emotions behind the anecdotes I shared.

Through his thoughtful questioning and genuine curiosity, he helped me unearth hidden memories and gain a deeper understanding of the chapters of my life. Working with Chris was not just productive but also fun and enlightening—a true collaboration that brought my story to life in ways I had never imagined.

Memoir writing, as I have come to realize, is an important and cathartic exercise. It allows us to reflect on our past, make sense of our present, and even glimpse into the future. Whether you choose to see your memoir published or keep it as a personal keepsake, the act of telling your own story holds immense value. It is a testament to your life, a way to honor the experiences that have shaped you, and a gift to yourself and those who will come after you.

Chris Epting's expertise as a memoirist shines through his approach to the craft. He understands the power of storytelling and the significance of capturing the essence of a life well-lived. His knowledge and experience in the genre are evident in the way he weaves narratives and evokes emotions.

In *Change of Seasons*, Chris skillfully guided me through the process of sharing my life's story with readers. His dedication, diligence, and genuine passion for the craft of writing were evident at every stage. I am grateful for his expertise, his friendship, and his ability to help me reveal the layers of my life.

Whether you are a seasoned writer or a first-time storyteller, Chris will be there to guide and inspire you, ensuring that your path of self-discovery is one that is both transformative and fulfilling.

> — **John Oates,** one-half of Hall & Oates and a member of the Songwriters Hall of Fame and the Rock & Roll Hall of Fame

PREFACE

I am thrilled to welcome you to my memoir-writing book. Whether you are a seasoned writer or just starting out, I believe that everyone has a story worth telling, and I hope that the tools and techniques shared in this book will inspire you to share your own unique story.

Writing a memoir is an incredibly rewarding and cathartic experience. It's a chance to reflect on our experiences, explore our emotions, and share our insights with others. But it can also be daunting. Many of us struggle with organizing our memories, opening up about our past, and finding our voice. That's where this book comes in.

In this book, I have shared my own experiences and knowledge gained over years of writing and teaching memoir. I have included exercises, prompts, and examples to guide you through the process of effectively telling your stories right through the process of publishing your collected work. My hope is that these tools will help you overcome writer's block, develop your writing skills, and gain the confidence you need to tell your story and share it with a broader audience.

Writing a memoir is not just about the technical aspects of writing. It is about the emotional journey of self-discovery and growth that comes with writing about your own life. It is about finding the courage to delve deep into your past, to relive memories and confront emotions that may have been buried for years. Through writing memoir, we can make sense of our lives, come to terms with our pasts, and create a deeper understanding of ourselves.

I believe that writing memoir is not only about personal growth but about giving back to society. Memoir allows us to document our unique experiences, perspectives, and insights that can enrich the lives of others. By sharing our stories, we can build bridges, foster empathy, and create a deeper understanding of the human experience. Beyond that, writing a memoir can leave a legacy for future generations. It is a way to preserve our stories and share them with our loved ones and generations to come. Our stories can inspire, educate, and entertain; they have a profound impact on the world around us.

So, whether you are writing for personal growth, to give back to society, or to create a legacy, I hope this book will inspire and guide you. I want to thank you for choosing to read this book and for allowing me to share my passion for memoir writing with you.

But before we truly get underway, I want to talk about John Cheever.

John Cheever was an American novelist and short story writer who was widely regarded as one of the most important writers of the 20th century. He was born on May 27, 1912, in Quincy, Massachusetts, and died on June 18, 1982, in Ossining, New York. Cheever's writing often focused on the lives of upper-middle-class Americans and their struggles with identity, morality, and the American Dream. His stories frequently explored themes of suburban life, family relationships, and the nature of human longing and desire. Cheever's most famous works include the novels *The Wapshot Chronicle* and *Falconer*, as well as the short story collections *The Enormous Radio and Other Stories* and *The Stories of John Cheever*. He was the recipient of numerous awards during his lifetime, including the Pulitzer Prize and the National Book Award. Cheever's writing is celebrated for its rich, evocative language, its deeply empathetic characters, and its ability to capture the complexities of human experience in all its joy and sorrow. He remains an influential figure in American literature.

Somehow, I got to know him when I was about twelve. In fact, he became my first writing mentor.

As I sat down to write this preface, I couldn't help but reflect on what has led me here. The book's title itself holds special significance for me. It's derived from a quote by Cheever: "For me a page of good prose is where one hears the rain. A page of good prose is when one hears the noise of battle.... A page of good prose seems to me the most serious dialogue that well-informed and intelligent men and women carry on today in their endeavor to make sure that the fires of this planet burn peaceably."

Being mentored by such a literary giant was a transformative experience. John Cheever not only imparted his wisdom on the craft of writing—he nurtured my passion for storytelling. His guidance and teachings became an essential part of my writing experience and are a driving force behind this book.

The inspiration for *Where One Hears the Rain* goes beyond my relationship with John Cheever. As a memoirist who has had the privilege of cowriting books with many fascinating individuals, I found myself drawn to the art of memoir writing. It was this fascination that led me to start a memoir workshop nearly a decade ago.

Over the years, watching my students embrace the power of personal storytelling has been an impactful learning experience. Their stories, their struggles, and their triumphs have taught me so much about the craft and the human experience. It is through their journeys that the idea for this book began to take shape.

The combination of writing alongside others, teaching aspiring writers (seeing some get published), and experiencing the joy of being published firsthand has ignited a deep inspiration within me. This inspiration has led me to chart a writing course aimed at creating a comprehensive roadmap—a guide that will empower you to find your voice, craft your unique story, and, if you so desire, navigate the path toward publication.

Everyone has different goals when it comes to writing a memoir. Some envision leaving behind a heartfelt collection of memories for their children or grandchildren to cherish. Others dream of seeing their name atop the illustrious *New York Times* bestseller list. And, of course, there are countless aspirations that fall anywhere along this vast spectrum. No matter where your personal goals lie, I firmly believe that the power of strong storytelling transcends everything else.

My hope is that these tools will help you overcome writer's block, develop your writing skills, and gain the confidence you need to tell your story and share it with a broader audience.

It is my fervent belief that everyone has a story worth telling, and this book is designed to guide and inspire you. Whether you are just starting to explore the idea of writing a memoir or have already begun, *Where One Hears the Rain* will serve as your trusted companion, providing encouragement, guidance, and actionable steps to bring your story into the world.

So, let's embrace the power of storytelling. Let our words flow onto the page and unleash the full potential of our stories. Whether your goal is personal or professional, ambitious or casual, let us remember that the act of writing itself is a transformative experience. Let us honor our stories, discover the depth of our voices, and celebrate the magic of sharing our narratives with the world.

It's time to unlock your creativity, find your writing rhythm, and begin this incredible journey. So, grab your pen, open your heart (and maybe your laptop!), and let's get writing. I'm ready. If you've gotten this far, I'd say you are too.

With that, here we go....

INTRODUCTION

I grew up in Westchester County, New York, in a town called Ossining. We lived in the rural part of the village on a winding, idyllic country lane called Spring Valley Road. (Other roads in the area were Hawkes Avenue, Apple Bee Farms Road, Cedar Lane...you get the idea.)

While it was isolated from things like supermarkets and shops (and people!), it did afford a unique experience through this dichotomy: while it was very much "country living" with lakes, woods, waterfalls, ponds, frogs, lizards, fishing, deer, nature trails (not to mention skating, sleigh riding, and shoveling icy steps in the winter while tossing rock salt), it was still just a scant forty-five minutes or so from New York City. So, while you might have been lazily fishing for sunnies and bluegills at three o'clock on a summer afternoon, that evening you could be at a Broadway show or a Mets game. A bright winter day spent clearing the lake to skate and play could end that night at Madison Square Garden watching the New York Rangers. All in all, it was an invigorating environment to grow up in.

This "best of both worlds" situation attracted notable people to the area. Jackie Gleason, for one. The fine actor Howard da Silva. Even Peter Frampton (on the heels of his blockbuster album *Frampton Comes Alive!*). They all escaped to these woods for solace, privacy, and the knowledge that New York City was easily within reach. But it was one neighbor in particular who made the biggest impression on me, and though I didn't fully realize it at the time, he was one of America's great authors.

I had decided early on that I wanted to be a writer. I had written a short story that truly impressed my fourth-grade teacher, Ms. Tina Rinaldi, to the point where she notified my parents and suggested they encourage me in this arena—and even mentioned it to a couple of other teachers. (Ms. Duff, my fifth grade teacher, I remember, got very excited.) For me, having a teacher become that invested in something I'd done was significant—and its effect lasts to this day. From that moment on, I was set. Come hell or high water, I was determined to be a writer. (A fallback I'd use many times when things like math grades suffered: "Hey...who needs math?... I'm gonna be a writer.")

My parents were fine with the fact that I wanted to be a writer by the time I was nine years old. A couple of years later, after watching me write regularly outside of school, my father suggested I take it a step further by dropping a note to a man who lived down the road—a writer named John Cheever—to see if he could offer me any advice. I had never heard of John Cheever, but I did know that my father had a couple of his books stacked on a shelf next to other famous authors, like Hemingway and Steinbeck. So I did. I wrote a few simple sentences to this man I'd never heard of, asking for some guidance. My mom drove me down Spring Valley Road (until it became

Cedar Lane) and I placed the note in a large silver mailbox clearly labeled "Cheever."

Then, just a few days later, I got a neatly typed note that has been committed to memory since I opened the envelope:

Dear Chris Epting:

It is nice to know that there is another writer living in the neighborhood. I will call you one day soon and then maybe we can take a walk and talk about writing.

(signed)
John Cheever

I could tell from my parents' reaction that this was a big deal. (There's something about seeing adults get genuinely excited, acting almost like kids, that impresses a young person. It feels incongruous, but in a good way.)

Several days after receiving his reply, the phone in our house rang. My mom said it was for me and I could tell from the look on her face that it was not one of my pals—John Mungo or Tommy Monohan—calling. She watched intently as I took the receiver.

"Hello?"

"Yes, Chris..." a rich, weathered, weary (vaguely British?) New England–accented voice began. "Hello, Chris. This is John Cheever."

With that, I was introduced to one of the greatest fiction writers in American literary history.

He asked me a few questions about what I liked to write. Short stories, I said. "So do I," he said, then asked if I might be able to come over to his home for a visit. (I remember thinking that, because Little League All-Stars was just underway, that it would be tough to get a visit in during practices.) But he spoke to my mom for a minute or so, and when she hung up, we had a plan. In just a couple of days, I was to be dropped off at his house after school for a visit. And I was to bring some writing samples.

Cheever lived in a beautiful colonial-style home. Nestled at 197 Cedar Lane, it held a rich history that seemed to reflect the literary brilliance that emanated from within its walls.

Originally constructed in 1795, it stood as a testament to the enduring charm of classic architecture. However, its true transformation came in the 1920s when the esteemed architect Eric Gugler lent his expertise to renovate the house. Gugler's name carried a weight of significance, considering he had left his mark on the Oval Office during the 1930s by working closely with President Franklin D. Roosevelt to redesign and reshape the iconic space. The very hands that had shaped the heart of American politics had also graced the Cheevers' house, giving it a touch of historical grandeur.

In 1961, coincidentally the year of my own birth, John Cheever became the fortunate owner of this remarkable dwelling. The house seemed to have chosen its occupants wisely, as if recognizing the creative spirit that resided within Cheever's being. As a writer, his words flowed effortlessly, painting vivid landscapes of human emotion, and the house became a sanctuary, nurturing his literary genius. Within those walls, Cheever crafted his stories, his imagination soaring freely, his pen breathing life into characters that would captivate people for generations to come. The house became a silent witness to the birth of literary masterpieces, each room carrying the echoes of inspiration and creativity.

To discover the house, you drove down a long, wooded cul-de-sac driveway, and a golden retriever (maybe it was an Irish setter) ran up to greet arriving visitors. My mom dropped me off, watching as Mr. Cheever met me at the door and invited me in. I immediately noticed the scent of wood smoke. I loved that. That magical aroma of fireplaces in old colonial houses infuses the air with a sense of warmth and history. The fragrance envelopes you, wraps you in a comforting embrace that transcends time, and carries the essence of crackling fires, hearths ablaze with flickering flames, and centuries-old fireplaces that have witnessed countless stories.

Mr. Cheever was a distinctive looking man. His long, drawn face had lots of lines and crevices in it. He seemed a bit tired and aloof, but also relaxed as he ambled into a very well-oiled den. After getting me a Coke, he motioned for me to sit down. It was a while before he said anything. Instead, he went across the room and started flipping through record albums until finally he found what he was looking for, held it up and said, "This is a remarkable album. Have you ever heard it?" I told him that yes, I was quite familiar with *Rubber Soul*, and seconds later, "I've Just Seen a Face" was coming out of his small stereo speakers. Later, when "Michelle" came on, he said he thought it was "absolutely incredible." He liked "In My Life" too.

Finally, he sat down. Then he arranged a row of about twenty cigarettes on the antique table next to him. For the next hour or so, as he finished one cigarette, he'd light up another one.

Cheever started with basic teacher/student questions. He asked me why I liked writing, what else I liked in life, how I liked school, and so on. I showed him some stories I'd brought along, and he said he'd hold on to them, read them, and then offer his critique when he was finished. He listened thoughtfully to me and took deep hits on his cigarettes, releasing ungodly amounts of blue smoke. After hearing about how much I liked playing baseball and that we were in our postseason as All-Stars, he got very interested, and I remember thinking, *Good, he's a baseball fan. We have a bit in common.*

As we neared what seemed to be the end of our discussion, he said he had a bit of advice. He said he didn't think people could be taught to write or led to write. Real writers write, period. If it's in you, you do it. So go home, he told me, and begin keeping a journal. Cheever said that journals force you to write, and that's what separates writers from people "who simply say they want to write." He said journals are where you develop your style and point of view. How you start creating a discipline for yourself. I said I'd start soon, and he said, "Start today. There's no point in waiting. Go home and start a journal. If you really want to write, then go home and write. And then, when you write something you think is important, I will look at it for you. We can meet like this from time to time, but you have to really want to write. It's a great deal of work, and you must be serious." (I remember this incident well because I did start a journal that day, and the first entry was a description of my first meeting with John Cheever.)

Mr. Cheever—as I addressed him from that point on— drove me home in his red Volkswagen Rabbit. As he pulled up our long driveway, I noticed my mom looking out the door off the kitchen. Getting out of the car, I asked, "Would you please get out and say hi to my mom? My folks are both huge fans of yours." He smiled, even laughed a bit, and said, "My pleasure." I left the two of them chatting in the driveway and went to find a blank pad of paper so I could start my journal.

A few weeks later, he called to invite me back to his home to review some of the work I'd left with him—and thus began a friendship that would last until his death in 1981. The years getting to know him were very special. From walks down Spring Valley Road to author readings in the local library, even calling an English professor I had in college to suggest I be allowed to take his much-worshipped course, John Cheever was very generous when it came to helping me with my writing. I still think about how lucky I was to have known someone so great, someone who took the time to share some stories and advice—someone who gave some critique and company to, as he put it, "another writer living in the neighborhood." But I'm also reminded of the many bits of information he gave me that are laced throughout this book. He may not have spoken to me about memoir per se, but good writing is good writing. Character development, conflict, resolution, powerful descriptions—those elements are important no matter the form or genre. I've always wanted to find a way to properly share the advice I was so generously given by this master, and so that's certainly part of what inspired this book.

John Cheever had a remarkable talent for crafting beautiful, evocative sentences that captured the nuances of the human experience. His prose was characterized by its elegance, clarity, and emotional resonance. He was able to create vivid, fully realized characters and settings with just a few well-chosen words. A master of the short story, he was able to condense complex narratives and themes into tight, powerful works of fiction that left a lasting impact on readers.

Cheever's work was marked by its honesty and compassion. He had a deep understanding of the human condition and was able to explore the complexities of human relationships and emotions with great sensitivity and insight. He was not afraid to confront difficult or uncomfortable truths, and his writing often revealed a deep sense of empathy and humanity. A keen observer of the world around him, Cheever's work often reflected the social and cultural changes that were taking place in America during the mid-20th century. His stories captured the anxieties and aspirations of the post-war generation, and his writing has been praised for its ability to capture the spirit of its time. In short, John Cheever was a great writer because of his talent for language and storytelling, his ability to empathize with his characters and his readers, and his capacity to capture the essence of his time and place in history. In this book, I will do my best to channel what I learned from him.

It starts, as I recall, with me eagerly listening one day as he shared some of his experiences teaching at the prestigious Iowa Writers' Workshop. Mr. Cheever spoke about how he would occasionally, while teaching at colleges, take aside young writers and ask them a simple but profound question: "Why are you here?" He explained that he was searching for a particular answer, one that set apart the truly dedicated and passionate writers from the rest. He told me that many aspiring writers would talk about their love for writing, their aspirations to become authors like him, and their excitement for the craft. However, he confessed that he wasn't interested in those answers. Instead, he listened intently for a different response. He wanted to hear some variation of, "I'm here because I have to write."

Mr. Cheever emphasized the significance of this distinction. He explained that when writing becomes a necessity—when it is as essential to one's being as eating, sleeping, or breathing—it sets writers apart. It becomes an integral part of their psyche, an ingrained compulsion that they cannot ignore or resist.

I was struck by the power of his words and the depth of insight they contained. It was a revelation for me as a young writer, as I began to understand that true dedication to the craft goes beyond mere passion. It is about an inner drive, an unyielding need to put words on paper, to express oneself through the written word. Since that conversation with John Cheever, I have never forgotten his description of the difference between wanting to write and having to write. It reminds me that writing is not just a hobby or a career choice; it is an integral part of who I am. In the end, it is this distinction that separates writers from one another—the understanding that writing is not just a choice but an imperative. And I am committed to living up to that distinction, to writing with the same sense of urgency and purpose that John Cheever so eloquently conveyed all those years ago. What really strikes me, as I sit here writing this book, is that I'm the same age that John Cheever was when I first contacted him. "Time," as a friend of mine says, "is a bizarre river."

As far as how I came to be a memoirist, it certainly wasn't by design. I am a nonfiction writer. I had written a number of books about travel, history, baseball, rock 'n' roll, and some other things I'm deeply passionate about. As a journalist, I was writing a lot about music and was becoming friendly with some of the subjects I was covering. One of those was a gentleman named Phil Collen, the lead guitarist for Def Leppard. Over a couple of years, Phil and his lovely wife Helen had become good friends of mine. One time at a show in San Diego, I broached the idea of writing his story with him. I'm not even sure what made me think of it in that moment, outside of just having the opportunity to personally witness what an interesting life he led. Phil was intrigued. We had some conversations about it, then we drafted a book proposal and sold it. That was the easy part. The hard part was sitting down and writing the book, which became *Adrenalized*.

I found the experience of writing with Phil rewarding, challenging, motivating, and quite satisfying overall. It was exhilarating to watch an accomplished creative artist like Phil discover his literary voice and then begin confronting serious truths about his life and his profession. At the end of the project, I knew I had discovered a new passion. Whatever else I might be writing at the time—be it books or articles—I knew that I also wanted to collaborate with other artists on their memoirs. Soon after Phil's book came out, I had a similar conversation with John Oates, who I had gotten to know after interviewing him a number of times. John initially dismissed the idea of writing a memoir, but after I described what the process had been like with Phil, his curiosity was piqued. We began work on the project soon after. John, a seasoned writer himself and former journalism student at Temple University, was an extremely engaged writing partner.

This book expands upon many cowriting experiences—not just with Phil Collen and John Oates, but many other subjects that I've been fortunate enough to write with—that I've ultimately learned a great deal from. Again, I'm an accidental memoirist. I never planned on this being part of my writing portfolio, but I'm incredibly thankful it is.

When someone hires you to write their memoir with them, they are entrusting you with their personal—and often deeply emotional—life events. This is a significant act of trust, as the memoirist is essentially inviting you into their life and asking you to help them tell their story in a way that accurately represents their vision. The trust that the memoirist places in you can be a humbling experience, as it reflects their confidence in your ability to capture the essence of their life and convey it in a way that is both engaging and respectful. It is important to honor this trust by being a compassionate and attentive listener, and by working collaboratively with the memoirist to ensure that their story is told in their own voice and in a way that accurately reflects what they have been through. In addition, it's important to recognize the responsibility that comes with this trust. As the writer, you have a duty to treat the memoirist's experiences with sensitivity and care, and to respect their privacy and boundaries throughout the writing process.

A couple of years after writing Phil's book, I realized that working with other people offered me a unique opportunity to learn more about the memoir writing process. Although each subject was completely different and brought with them their own unique set of experiences, dreams, desires, and disciplines, there were definitely patterns in terms of process. So I began teaching a memoir workshop in Huntington Beach, California, where I lived at the time. With each session, the workshops became more and more popular. Soon I was asked to teach at a variety of places throughout Orange County, and then eventually—once the pandemic hit—online through Zoom. To date,

I have had the unique opportunity and privilege to lead workshops with thousands of writers from all over the world.

There are several reasons why I enjoy teaching a memoir class. I'm passionate about writing and storytelling, so teaching a memoir class allows me to share my knowledge and enthusiasm with others. I'm able to introduce my students to the joys of writing and help them discover their own unique voice and style.

Helping others matters too. Teaching a memoir class is a rewarding experience, as I get to help my students explore their personal experiences, memories, and emotions, and guide them in crafting their stories. I find it fulfilling to see students grow as writers and gain confidence in their abilities.

I view this book as an opportunity for us to work together on a personal, one-to-one level, allowing me to channel and harness all that I have learned so that you may also benefit from it.

I am deeply grateful that you are reading this now. If you're ready to get started, I know I am.

CHAPTER 1

Where to Begin?

Introductions. Before we get into this book, I'd like to take a moment to get to know each other. Just as I would in a memoir workshop, I invite you to introduce yourself and reflect on why you are here, what your goals are, and what you hope to achieve.

Are you that person whom others have told, "You *have* to write a book"? Do you have a secret that you've been longing to share with the world? Or perhaps you're driven by the desire to leave behind stories of love and learning for your family members? Take a moment to think about why you are reading this book and why you want to write.

If I were to call on you in class to answer that question, what would you say? What inspires you in this moment? It's valuable to document your thoughts and motivations, as they serve as a testament to what drives you.

Writing a book can be fueled by a multitude of reasons. It may be a means of self-expression, allowing you to communicate your unique perspective and voice. It can offer catharsis, helping you explore emotions, heal from past traumas, or make sense of complex life events. Writing can also be a way to share knowledge, inspire others, or leave a lasting legacy for your loved ones or future generations.

Some may feel compelled to write in order to advocate for social change, raise awareness about important issues, or give a voice to marginalized communities. For others, writing is simply a passion—a creative outlet that brings fulfillment and allows for the exploration of personal experiences or literary techniques.

Each of us has a unique story to tell, and our reasons for writing differ.

What are some reasons people write a memoir?

1. To find some kind of meaning and order in an often chaotic world
2. To discover who you really are by confronting the truth(s) of your life
3. To re-witness the most vital stages of your life
4. To overcome fear, guilt, shame, and regret
5. To preserve your family's history
6. To improve your ability to communicate
7. To build self-esteem
8. To figure out who you are
9. To become a better thinker
10. To learn how to forgive yourself
11. To set the record straight
12. To confess something
13. To heal or process past experiences
14. To inspire or motivate others

Why do *you* want to write a memoir? Perhaps...

1. You're an authority in your field
2. You have a powerful, unique story to share
3. You want to understand or know yourself better
4. You want to document your life
5. You enjoy a challenge
6. You relish playing with language
7. You find writing therapeutic
8. You can't help but write

As we start, let's embrace the power of storytelling, the importance of human connection, and the potential for personal growth and understanding that can come from sharing and listening to each other's stories. Remember, this is your moment to reflect on your own motivations and inspirations for writing. Embrace the power of your voice and the stories you have to share.

SO, WHAT EXACTLY IS A "STORY"?

Storytelling is the act of sharing a narrative through oral or written means with the purpose of entertaining, informing, inspiring, or educating an audience. Stories can take many different forms and can be fictional or about real-life events.

At its core, storytelling involves creating a narrative that captures the attention and imagination of the audience, using elements such as characters, setting, plot, and conflict to convey a message or theme. Storytelling can be found in many different forms, including literature, film, theater, music, visual art, and more.

In addition to being a means of entertainment and creative expression, storytelling has also been used throughout history as a way of passing down cultural traditions, preserving history, and sharing knowledge and wisdom. Storytelling can help us connect with others, understand different perspectives and experiences, and gain insight into ourselves and the world around us.

Storytelling is important for many reasons, both on an individual and societal level. Stories help us connect with others by sharing experiences, emotions, and ideas. When we hear or tell stories, we can find common ground with others and develop a sense of empathy and understanding. Stories are a powerful means of communication, allowing us to convey complex information and emotions in a way that is easy to understand and remember. Stories can also help us persuade and influence others, whether in personal or professional contexts.

Stories can also help us define our individual and collective identities. They can shape our beliefs, values, and sense of self, and provide us with a sense of belonging and purpose. Stories can even be healing, allowing us to process difficult emotions and experiences. They can help us find meaning and hope in challenging situations, and offer comfort and solace during times of grief or trauma.

And, of course, storytelling is a creative art form that allows us to explore new ideas, experiment with different perspectives and techniques, and express ourselves in unique and innovative ways.

Storytelling plays a vital role in human communication, culture, and society. Whether we are sharing personal experiences with friends, reading a novel, or listening to a podcast, storytelling helps us connect with others, understand the world around us, and find meaning and purpose in our lives.

There are many different kinds of storytelling that can help your writing, each with their own unique characteristics and styles. Here are a few examples:

Oral storytelling: Oral storytelling involves sharing stories through spoken word, often in a live performance setting. This can include traditional folktales, personal narratives, and other types of stories.

Digital storytelling: Digital storytelling involves using multimedia tools—such as video, audio, images, and interactive elements—to tell a story. This can include online videos, podcasts, and interactive websites.

Visual storytelling: Visual storytelling involves using images and graphics to convey a story. This can include comics, graphic novels, and other types of illustrated narratives.

Performance storytelling: Performance storytelling combines elements of oral and visual storytelling, often involving live performance with spoken word, music, and other artistic elements.

Interactive storytelling: Interactive storytelling involves the audience participating in the story, often through choose-your-own-adventure style narratives or other interactive elements.

Storytelling is a diverse and constantly evolving art form that takes many different shapes and forms. Whether through spoken word, written text, or digital media, storytelling remains a powerful means of sharing experiences, emotions, and ideas with others.

Now, let's start with the basics. What is a memoir?

Simply stated, a memoir is a type of nonfiction that focuses on a particular period, theme, or experience in the author's life. While other nonfiction books, such as biographies or autobiographies, may also focus on a person's life story, there are several key differences that set memoirs apart:

Narrow focus: Memoirs tend to focus on a particular aspect of the author's life, such as a specific experience or period of time. In contrast, biographies or autobiographies may cover an entire lifetime or career.

Subjectivity: Memoirs are often written in the first person and reflect the author's personal perspective and experiences. This can create a more subjective and emotional tone than other types of nonfiction.

Storytelling: Memoirs use storytelling techniques, such as dialogue and scene setting, to create a narrative arc and engage readers. This makes them more similar to works of fiction than other types of nonfiction.

Emphasis on reflection: Memoirs often emphasize the author's reflection on their experiences and the lessons they have learned. This introspective quality sets them apart from other nonfiction books that may focus more on facts or events.

A memoir is a personal and subjective account of a particular aspect of the author's life, told in a storytelling format with an emphasis on reflection and introspection. Memoirs can be factual or based on real events, but they may also incorporate fictional elements to help convey the author's message or to enhance the storytelling. The primary goal of a memoir is to share a meaningful or impactful personal story with readers.

I've come to appreciate the importance of focusing on a specific period or event in one's life when writing a memoir. It's crucial for writers to understand that they're not attempting to cover their entire life story within the pages of their memoir. Instead, they should aim to capture the essence and significance of a particular timeframe or thematic meaning.

A wonderful example that I often share with my students is the book *My Week with Marilyn*. The book—which was made into a good film in 2011—was written by Colin Clark and published in 2000. It is a memoir that recounts the author's experiences during the summer of 1956 when he worked as an assistant on the set of *The Prince and the Showgirl* starring Marilyn Monroe and Sir Laurence Olivier. The memoir provides an intimate and behind-the-scenes look at the interactions between the author, Monroe, and other notable figures involved in the production. It captures the author's personal observations, interactions, and reflections on Monroe's behavior, insecurities, and the challenges she faced during the filming process. *My Week with Marilyn* offers a unique perspective on Monroe's life and the complexities of fame.

In this memoir, the author vividly describes the tumultuous and unforgettable week he spent with Monroe. While the action unfolds within that one-week timeframe, it's important to note that the story is not confined to those seven days.

WHAT MAKES MEMOIR SUCH A UNIQUE GENRE?

Memoirs are inherently unique in the world of prose, and there are a few reasons why:

Human connection: Memoirs provide us with a deep and personal connection to the author's experiences. Readers can relate to the author's struggles, triumphs, and emotions, which can help readers feel less alone.

Insight: Memoirs can provide insight into different perspectives and experiences. Reading about someone else's life can broaden our understanding of the world and help us develop empathy and compassion for others.

Authenticity: Memoirs are based on the author's personal experiences and emotions, making memoirs more compelling to readers.

Connection: Memoirs are often deeply personal and emotional, which can create a sense of connection and empathy between the audience and the writer. People can see themselves reflected in the writer's experiences and find comfort and inspiration in their stories.

Entertainment: Memoirs can be entertaining, much like a novel or a movie. Memoirists use storytelling techniques to keep us interested and invested in their stories.

Diversity: Memoirs offer a diverse range of perspectives and experiences that may not be represented in mainstream media. They can highlight marginalized voices and bring attention to issues that are often ignored.

Empowerment: Writing a memoir can be an empowering experience for writers, as they are able to tell their story in their own words and on their own terms. It can also be empowering for readers, as they see someone else triumphing over challenges and find their own strength and resilience.

Education: Memoirs can be educational and informative, providing insight into different cultures, experiences, and perspectives. They can also shed light on important historical events or social issues.

Self-help: Many memoirs explore themes of personal growth, overcoming obstacles, and finding purpose and meaning in life. Readers can learn from the author's experiences and apply those lessons to their own lives.

Generally, memoirs are popular because they offer readers a unique perspective on life, provide human connection, and are often both insightful and entertaining. Audiences are drawn to memoirs because they appreciate the honesty of memoirists who share their personal stories with the world. There are countless memoirs that have been written over the years, and it's challenging to narrow down the best, but here are a few of the most highly regarded memoirs of all time:

Night by Elie Wiesel: Wiesel's memoir recounts his experiences in Nazi concentration camps during World War II.

The Glass Castle by Jeannette Walls: This memoir tells the story of Walls's unconventional childhood and her relationship with her eccentric parents.

Angela's Ashes by Frank McCourt: This memoir details the author's impoverished upbringing in Ireland and his struggles with poverty, alcoholism, and loss.

Wild by Cheryl Strayed: Strayed's memoir follows her journey hiking the Pacific Crest Trail after the death of her mother.

Born a Crime by Trevor Noah: This memoir by comedian and TV host Trevor Noah explores his experiences growing up in South Africa during apartheid.

Educated by Tara Westover: This memoir recounts Westover's upbringing in a strict and abusive household and her goal to receive an education.

I'm Glad My Mom Died by Jennette McCurdy: This memoir is about McCurdy's career as a child actress and her difficult relationship with her abusive mother.

There are also many famous literary writers who have written memoirs. Here are a few examples:

I Know Why the Caged Bird Sings by Maya Angelou

A Moveable Feast by Ernest Hemingway

The Year of Magical Thinking by Joan Didion

On Writing: A Memoir of the Craft by Stephen King

Notes of a Native Son by James Baldwin

These authors have used their experiences, memories, and emotions to craft compelling and powerful memoirs.

THE CHALLENGES OF WRITING A MEMOIR

Writing a memoir can be a daunting and emotional process. Here are some of the biggest challenges writers face:

Emotional vulnerability: Writing a memoir requires sharing deeply personal experiences. This can be difficult, as it often involves revisiting painful memories or feelings.

Objectivity: It can be difficult to maintain objectivity when writing about personal experiences. Writers often struggle with finding the right balance between personal perspective and objective storytelling.

Memory accuracy: Memories can be unreliable, and it can be difficult to remember specific details accurately. Writers may need to rely on outside sources, such as journals or interviews with others, to fill in gaps or clarify details.

Legal and ethical considerations: Writing about real people and events can raise legal and ethical concerns, particularly if it involves liability defamation. Writers need to be aware of the potential consequences of their writing and take steps to protect themselves and others.

Organization and structure: Memoirs require a clear structure and narrative arc to tell a compelling story. Writers may struggle with organizing their memories and experiences into a coherent and entertaining narrative.

Reader engagement: Memoirs need to be relatable. Writers need to consider their audience and ensure that their story resonates with readers.

Writing a memoir requires skill, emotional intelligence, and attention to detail. By anticipating these challenges and taking steps to address them, writers can create a powerful memoir.

A BRIEF HISTORY OF MEMOIRS

Memoirs are one of the most popular genres of literature, offering readers an intimate glimpse into the lives and experiences of others. While memoirs may seem like a relatively new phenomenon, the truth is that they have been around for centuries, evolving and changing along with the literary landscape. History is an exciting subject for me, so I wanted to explore the history of memoir writing from its earliest beginnings to the present day.

The roots of memoir can be traced back to ancient times, when people would record their personal experiences and observations on scrolls or tablets. One of the earliest examples comes from the Greek historian and soldier Xenophon, who wrote *Anabasis* in the 4th century BCE. *Anabasis* is a memoir of Xenophon's experiences as a soldier in the Persian Expedition, and is considered one of the earliest surviving examples of the genre.

In the Middle Ages, memoir writing became more prevalent among religious figures, who used the genre as a way to record their spiritual quests and experiences. One of the most famous examples of this type of memoir is *The Confessions of Saint Augustine*, written at the end of the 4th century CE. Augustine's *Confessions* is a deeply personal and introspective work in which he reflects on his sinful past and his eventual conversion to Christianity.

During the Renaissance, memoir writing began to take on a more secular tone, with writers using the genre to record their experiences in the world of politics, art, and science. One of the most famous memoirs from this period is *The Autobiography of Benvenuto Cellini*, written in the 16th century. Cellini was a renowned artist and goldsmith, and his memoir offers readers a fascinating glimpse into Renaissance art and culture.

The 18th and 19th centuries saw a proliferation of memoir writing, as more and more people began to record their personal experiences and observations. One of the most famous memoirs from this period is *The Life of Samuel Johnson*, written by James Boswell in the late 18th century. Boswell's *Life* is a sprawling, multi-volume work that offers readers an intimate look at the life and times of one of England's most famous literary figures.

In the 20th century, memoir writing underwent a significant transformation as writers began to experiment with the genre and push its boundaries in new and exciting ways. One of the most famous examples of this is *The Autobiography of Alice B. Toklas*, written by Gertrude Stein in 1933. *Toklas* is not actually Stein's autobiography, but rather a memoir of Toklas's life with Stein written from Toklas's perspective. The book is a revolutionary work that challenges traditional notions of memoir and offers a unique and unconventional look at the lives of two of the most famous writers of the 20th century.

The 1960s and 1970s saw a surge in memoir writing, as writers like James Baldwin and Maya Angelou began to explore their personal experiences in their work. The rise of the feminist movement and the civil rights movement also helped to popularize the genre, with writers using their personal experiences to shed light on larger societal issues.

In the 1990s and 2000s, memoirs became even more popular, with books like Frank McCourt's *Angela's Ashes*, Mary Karr's *The Liars' Club*, and Elizabeth Gilbert's *Eat, Pray, Love* topping bestseller lists. Today, memoirs continue to be popular, with writers from all walks of life exploring their personal experiences in their work.

The art has continued to evolve and change, with writers experimenting with form, structure, and style in exciting new ways. One of the most notable examples of this is *Fun Home*, a graphic memoir written by Alison Bechdel and published in 2006. *Fun Home* is a deeply personal and introspective work that explores Bechdel's relationship with her father and her own sexuality. The book's use of graphic novel–style illustrations adds a visual dimension to the memoir, creating a unique and powerful reading experience.

Memoir writing has a rich and varied history, spanning centuries and encompassing a wide range of styles and forms. From the ancient scrolls of Xenophon to the graphic memoirs of today, it has always been a way for individuals to record their personal experiences and observations, then share them with others. Throughout the centuries, memoirs have provided readers with intimate glimpses into the lives and experiences of people from all walks of life, from religious figures to artists to soldiers to everyday people.

And now you're about to join the fray!

A JOHN CHEEVER MEMORY

When John Cheever's novel *Falconer* was released, I happened to be at his house for one of our writing sessions. As we sat in his study surrounded by books and typewriters, he handed me a copy of his latest work and signed it with a personal message. "See what you think of it," he said with a hint of anticipation in his voice. I was honored to receive such a gift from a literary master and couldn't wait to dive into its pages.

That night, I curled up in a cozy armchair and began reading. From the very first sentence, I was captivated by Cheever's lyrical prose and the depth of his storytelling. The novel is a gripping exploration of the human condition, delving into themes of redemption, isolation, and the search for freedom.

The story revolves around Ezekiel Farragut, a university professor who is serving time in Falconer State Prison for the murder of his brother. As the narrative unfolds, we witness Farragut's struggles with the harsh reality of prison life, his personal demons, and his quest for a sense of purpose and meaning. Cheever's writing is masterful in its ability to evoke a sense of introspection and emotional resonance. Through richly drawn characters and vivid descriptions, he immerses the audience into the claustrophobic world of the prison, with its intricate power dynamics and the inmates' desperate yearning for escape.

Amidst the grim setting, *Falconer* explores the complexities of human relationships. Farragut forms connections with fellow inmates, each with their own stories of despair and resilience. Their interactions highlight the universal longing for connection and understanding, even in the most unlikely of circumstances.

As I turned the pages, I found myself drawn deeper into the psychological and philosophical depths of the novel. Cheever's exploration of Farragut's inner turmoil, his contemplation of mortality, and his search for redemption hit me on a deep level. The book takes deep dives into themes of identity, guilt, and the possibility of transformation, leaving the audience with lingering questions about the nature of human existence. I may not have been familiar with John Cheever when I first started meeting with him in 1975, but reading this novel definitely gave me a sense of his greatness. I looked at him differently whenever I saw him from that point on. I was finally beginning to understand who he was.

Falconer received widespread acclaim for its lyrical prose, nuanced characterization, and thought-provoking themes. It is a testament to Cheever's mastery as a storyteller, showcasing his ability to weave together a tale that is both deeply personal and universally resonant.

During the height of his fame following the success of *Falconer*, Cheever's celebrity status reached its pinnacle. He embarked on extensive travels to distant destinations such as Russia and Bulgaria. Every now and then, amidst his adventures, I would find myself pleasantly surprised by the arrival of manila envelopes containing my own little stories, adorned with his personal notes scribbled in the margins.

CHAPTER 2

Why Is Memoir so Popular?

Memoir is becoming one of the fastest-growing literary genres for several reasons.

First, memoirs offer readers a personal connection to the author's life story. We are often drawn to memoirs because we want to understand how the author has dealt with the challenges they have faced in their own lives.

Second, memoirs are often seen as more authentic than other forms of writing because they are based on the author's own experiences. This can help people connect with the author and the story on a deeper level.

Third, memoirs offer a wide range of perspectives on life experiences, including those that may be underrepresented in other forms of literature. Memoirs can help us gain a better understanding of different cultures, lifestyles, and experiences. Memoirs also often dive into the psychological aspects of the author's experiences, such as their emotions, thoughts, and motivations. This can help readers gain insight into their own psychological processes and how they deal with challenging situations.

Finally, memoirs often focus on the growth and transformation of the author over time. People may find inspiration in the author's journey and learn valuable lessons about their own personal growth.

HEALTH BENEFITS OF MEMOIR WRITING

Yes, this can be good for you! Writing a memoir can be a therapeutic experience for some people. Here are some potential benefits of memoir writing:

Promotes self-reflection: Writing can help individuals gain a better understanding of their experiences, beliefs, and values. This process of self-reflection can be a powerful tool for personal growth and healing.

Offers a sense of closure: Writing can help you make sense of past experiences and find closure. By revisiting past events and emotions, individuals can process their feelings and gain a sense of resolution.

Catharsis: Writing about difficult or painful experiences can be cathartic, allowing you to express emotions that you may have suppressed or ignored. This can help you to release pent-up emotions and move toward healing.

Perspective: Writing your story can help you gain perspective on your life experiences, providing a broader context for your memories and allowing you to see how different events and relationships fit together. This process can help you to develop a more nuanced understanding of your life and the people and events that have shaped it.

Connection: Sharing your memoir with others can create a sense of connection and community. Knowing that others have experienced similar challenges or emotions can be validating and may help you feel less alone.

Provides a sense of control: Writing a memoir can help individuals take control of their story and their narrative. By sharing their experiences in their own words, individuals can assert their agency and reclaim their power.

Encourages empathy: Writing a memoir can help individuals develop empathy for themselves and others. By examining their own experiences, individuals may gain a better understanding of others' experiences and be more compassionate toward themselves and others.

Offers a creative outlet: Writing a memoir can be a creative and expressive outlet for individuals. It allows them to tell their story in their own voice and to experiment with different writing styles and techniques.

Writing a memoir can be a way to process and make sense of your past experiences and emotions, and can provide a sense of closure or healing. It can also be a way to share your story with others and provide inspiration or insight into your life.

TYPES OF MEMOIRS

There are several different kinds of memoirs that you can choose to write:

Personal: This form focuses on the author's personal experiences, often covering a specific period of time in their life.

Travel: A travel memoir recounts the author's experiences and observations during their travels. These memoirs often focus on specific destinations or cultures.

Historical: This approach focuses on a particular event or period in history, and often provides insights into the author's experiences and the broader cultural and societal context.

Loss: This type of memoir deals with the author's experience of grief, often after the death of a loved one.

Illness: These stories focus on the author's experiences with illness, recovery, and healing. They often explore themes of resilience, faith, and hope.

Food: These memoirs focus on the author's relationship with food and cooking, can include recipes and descriptions of meals, and may explore the role of food in their life and culture.

Coming-of-age: This kind of story focuses on the author's experiences growing up. They often explore themes of identity, family, and self-discovery.

Addiction: These focus on the author's struggles with addiction, recovery, and the effects of addiction on their life and relationships.

INITIAL FEARS

Writing a memoir is a deeply personal experience, so it's natural to feel anxious about it. Here are some common fears that writers experience when beginning a memoir:

Fear of judgment: Writing a memoir means sharing personal experiences and emotions with the world, which can be scary if you're worried about what others might think or how they might react.

Fear of backlash: Depending on the subject matter, you may be worried about negative reactions or criticism from people in your life.

Being vulnerable: Writing a memoir requires you to share personal details about your life, which can be intimidating. It's natural to feel anxious about sharing your innermost thoughts and feelings with others, especially if you fear judgment or rejection.

Revisiting painful experiences: Writing about difficult or traumatic experiences can be emotionally challenging and can summon intense emotions. It's important to approach this process with self-compassion and to take breaks as needed to avoid becoming overwhelmed.

Writing a memoir requires a high level of creativity and skill, which can be daunting. It's normal to feel anxious about conveying your experiences and emotions in a way that will attract readers. Writing about personal experiences—especially traumatic ones—can be emotionally challenging and can make you feel exposed. And, of course, there's the fear of not being a good writer. If you're not confident in your writing abilities, you may feel like you're not capable of telling your story in a way that's engaging or meaningful.

So yes, writing a memoir can be a scary and intimidating process. Despite these challenges, writing a memoir can also be a rewarding and transformative experience.

I want to emphasize the importance of *your* truth when it comes to memoir writing. Your experiences, emotions, and memories are unique to you; they form the foundation of your perspective, and they matter. However, it is crucial to also understand that your truth is subjective, and is shaped by your individual vantage point.

As you start writing, remember that your truth—as best as you remember it—is what matters. Memoir allows for the creative exploration of nonfiction, giving you the freedom to present your story from your unique perspective. Embrace this freedom, for it is what makes memoir such a captivating and deeply personal genre.

Within this genre of creative nonfiction, we embrace the notion that truth is subjective. Your memories may be influenced by time, emotions, and the personal lens through which you view the world. It is perfectly valid to present your truth as you remember it, even if it differs from the recollections of others who were part of your experience. Just remember that your truth is not about distorting facts or deliberately misrepresenting reality; rather, it's about embracing the nuances and complexities of your personal experiences, including the emotions, thoughts, and significance attached to them. Authenticity and vulnerability are the cornerstones of memoir writing.

Grant yourself permission to remember your past as best you can. Memory is a delicate vessel, and the passage of time may shape and blur its contents. Your task is to dive deep into the recesses of your recollections, mining the rich veins of your past, and piecing together the mosaic of your life as truthfully as you can. By embracing your truth, you honor your unique voice and perspective. Your story becomes a gateway that invites readers into your world—your joys, sorrows, triumphs, and tribulations. Your truth has the power to forge connections, stir empathy, and foster understanding.

PERSONAL NOTE

In 2010, I released my book *Hello, It's Me: Dispatches from a Pop Culture Junkie*. It's a memoir that unpacks various stories from my life that have affected me, many of which revolve around popular culture. However, I wanted to go beyond just sharing my perspective. So, for each story, I located someone connected—directly or indirectly—to the topic I was writing about and asked them to contribute a companion piece from their perspective. This approach added depth and richness to my book, providing diverse viewpoints and experiences.

One particular story revolves around the popular early 1970s song "Brandy" by Looking Glass, which had a huge impact on my twin sister and me. To shed more light on this song's significance, I tracked down Elliot Lurie, the singer and songwriter, who'd evolved into a successful record company executive. He graciously agreed to contribute a lovely essay reflecting on how the song had affected him.

By incorporating these companion pieces, my book aimed to capture a more comprehensive understanding of the influence of popular culture on our lives. It was a fascinating process that allowed me to connect with people who played a significant role in shaping the experiences I wrote about.

WORKING WITH JOHN OATES

Collaborating with John Oates on his memoir was an incredibly fascinating experience. One of the things that struck me the most was John's insistence that the book should not attempt to tell the story of Hall & Oates as a collective entity. Instead, he emphasized that he and Daryl had their own experiences and perspectives, and it was important to honor that individuality. John made it clear that he couldn't write for someone else.

We focused on John's personal experiences, particularly as they related to his journey within Hall & Oates. While the book certainly touched upon the duo's story, it was filtered through John's lens, providing a deeply personal and revealing perspective. Through his narrative, we analyzed the dynamics of the duo, their creative process, and the challenges they faced.

By centering the narrative on John's experiences, we were able to offer people a more intimate and authentic portrayal of Hall & Oates. It wasn't an exclusion of Daryl or the duo's story, but a different way of exploring their partnership. John's perspective added a layer of depth and richness to the narrative, allowing readers to connect with the duo on a more personal level.

But there was an early lesson to be learned. When writing memoir, especially in the early phases, it's common to hold back and not reveal the personal details and observations that can truly help bring a story to life. When I was first working with John, I sensed that he was resisting the urge to expose certain truths from his life. But he wasn't aware of it. In his mind, he was comfortable with the level of descriptive storytelling that we were collaborating on. I would occasionally meet John on the road when he was touring. Often times, musical artists have lots of downtime on the road to do things like work on a book, and John was no different. We were in a Las Vegas hotel suite spending the afternoon working on his memoir. As always, his VIP suite featured a lavish fruit basket that had been delivered by the local concert promoter. These were unlike any fruit baskets you and I will probably ever see in our lifetimes. We're talking—in some cases—a basket or some other form of container five feet tall, featuring exotic treats from all over the world. This particular time, I sat across from him on a couch with the massive basket between us.

"Look at the basket," I said to him. "What do you see?"

He laughed and said, "I see an incredibly expensive collection of rare and delicious fruit that I can't wait to dig into."

"It reminds me of this book we're working on," I replied. He stared at me quizzically, so I continued. "Everything looks amazing in there, doesn't it? The pineapples, guavas, the papayas… everything looks delectable. But we can't quite get to it because it's covered in red cellophane. It looks amazing, but until we get rid of the cellophane, there's no way we can truly enjoy it for what it is." I continued, "This is where we are right now in terms of this book. Everything looks wonderful, but you've got it all wrapped up in bright red cellophane. If you want the reader to truly be able to dig in and enjoy the stories, we need to remove the cellophane and experience everything firsthand."

John raised his eyebrows and said, "I get it. I completely understand. I've had a transparent barrier up around my truth. Psychologically, I've definitely placed it there for a reason… but now I need to remove it in order for us to do what we need to do."

From that day forward, whenever we started writing a new story, John always made a point to say, "Let's get rid of the cellophane. Let's really dig into this the way it needs to be written."

Sometimes the simplest metaphor can offer the deepest lesson when it comes to writing memoir.

CHAPTER 3

Three Concepts of Mine

As you begin, it's important for you to be honest with your audience. When memoirists are honest and transparent about their experiences, readers can trust them and connect with their stories on a deeper level. They appreciate the courage it takes to share personal stories, and they are more likely to engage with memoirs that feel genuine and authentic. In this chapter, we will explore three concepts I've developed that have not only shaped my own writing journey but have also proven invaluable in helping many other aspiring memoirists in my workshops bring honesty, depth, and resonance to their personal narratives.

1. THE INSTAGRAM EFFECT

I often refer to what I call the "Instagram effect." As a budding memoirist, I remember wondering how much I was allowed to enhance the stories I was writing about. It's a bit like applying filters to a photograph on Instagram. The actual photo, just like the actual event, doesn't change…but we can alter it slightly to bring out the effects that we remember.

I've come to understand that as memoirists, we're not writing as journalists—we're crafting as creative writers. We have the freedom to add color, dimension, and texture to our narratives as long as it's in line with the emotions we associate with those events. Memoir writing is about capturing the essence of our memories and bringing them to life in the way we remember them best.

When we think about memoirs, we often think about the raw truth as a faithful representation of events. However, while memoirs are based on real experiences, they are not purely objective accounts. They are filtered through our subjective lens, shaped by our memories, emotions, and perspectives. Just as an Instagram filter enhances the visual impact of a photograph, we, as memoirists, have the power to enhance the emotional impact of our stories.

Adding emotional power to our memoirs is perfectly acceptable, as long as we don't change the facts about the events themselves. It's not about distorting the truth; it's about infusing our stories with the depth and feeling that make them resonate with readers. Just like applying a filter to a photograph doesn't change the subject matter, adding descriptive language, personal reflections, and sensory details doesn't alter the core events of our memoirs. Instead, it creates a more immersive experience.

To achieve this, we can employ various literary techniques. We can dive into the rich tapestry of our memories and extract the vivid details—the sights, sounds, smells, tastes, and textures—that bring our stories to life. By evoking the sensory elements associated with a particular event, we transport the audience into our world, allowing them to experience the emotions we felt and the atmosphere we encountered.

We can also tap into our emotional reservoirs and explore the depth of our feelings. Memoirs are not just a recollection of events; they are emotional journeys. By expressing our authentic emotional responses, we allow readers to connect with us on a deep level. We can convey the elation, heartbreak, joy, or despair we experienced and paint a more nuanced and evocative picture of our lives.

As memoirists, we strive for truth and transparency. The fundamental events you're transcribing and their sequence should remain unchanged, as they form the backbone of our narratives. By weaving in our subjective experiences and perceptions, we can convey the significance of the events as we remember them, which in turn offers a more insightful reading experience.

Memoirs are not just about facts; they are about truth. The truth lies not only in the objective events, but also in the emotional truth that resonates within us. It's about capturing the essence of our experiences, the lessons we've learned, and the transformations we've undergone. By infusing our stories with personal reflections, introspection, and contemplative insights, we invite readers to take part in a shared exploration of the human condition.

The "Instagram effect" allows us to enhance the emotional impact and create a more vivid narrative without altering the factual events. It provides us with the creative freedom to add layers of depth and meaning to our stories.

However, it's important to acknowledge that walking this line between truth and embellishment can be challenging. As we strive to evoke the power of our memories, we must remain mindful of the boundaries. We shouldn't succumb to the temptation of fabricating or distorting facts to suit our desired narrative. Honesty and integrity should always guide our writing process.

To strike the right balance, we can rely on thorough research and meticulous fact-checking. By cross-referencing our memories with available resources—such as diaries, photographs, and conversations with others involved—we can ensure the accuracy of the factual details. This diligent approach allows us to weave the necessary emotional threads while maintaining the authenticity of our memoirs.

Additionally, we can draw inspiration from other literary genres. Techniques employed in fiction—such as storytelling devices, vivid descriptions, and dialogue—can enrich our memoirs and make them more engaging. By blending elements of fiction with the truth of our experiences, we enhance the narrative flow and captivate readers in a way that pure factual accounts may not achieve.

Ultimately, the "Instagram effect" reminds us that our stories are not mere recitations of events but powerful vehicles for emotional connection and shared understanding. By embracing the artistry of memoir writing, we can craft narratives that have emotional depth, as well as the power to inspire and uplift others.

All that said, consider the "Instagram effect" as you weave your memories into captivating stories that illuminate the human experience. Honor the truth of your past while infusing your narratives with the richness of emotions, the allure of descriptive language, and the transformative power of personal reflection. In doing so, you open the door to where the past comes alive, and your story becomes a testament to the beauty and complexity of the human spirit.

2. THE POWER OF PLACE

In my writing experiences, I've discovered something truly extraordinary—something I call "the power of place." As an author who has written at length about travel and exploration, I've had the privilege of documenting historic events and unraveling their mysteries by seeking out the precise locations where they unfolded. From the profound to the whimsical, I've written numerous books chronicling these adventures where I return to the exact sites where things both great and small took place.

For me, there is an undeniable magic that occurs when you start on a quest to find that exact spot. It's as if the act of physically standing in the place where history was made forges an unbreakable connection to the event itself. This phenomenon, I believe, is akin to the experience of writing a memoir. Revisiting the sites that hold personal significance throughout our lives allows us to rekindle our connection with those pivotal moments. Whether it's a playground or baseball field, a childhood home or a cherished classroom, returning to these places holds the power to unlock memories in the most extraordinary manner. I cannot stress enough the importance of this practice whenever it is feasible.

Among my own expeditions, one stands out as particularly important. In 2009, I brought my family to John Cheever's house. Though he had passed away many years prior, his wife, Mary, was still alive, and she graciously hosted us for one unforgettable afternoon. At the time, I was engrossed in writing my memoir, and whenever possible, I returned to the very locations where the stories of my life unfolded.

The experience of visiting John Cheever's house was nothing short of transformative. In the presence of Mary, I felt a tangible connection to the essence of my past experiences there. It was as if the walls whispered stories and the air held the echoes of his words. This encounter left an indelible mark on me. It served as a reminder of the impact that revisiting significant places can have on our writing. It bridged the gap between author and subject, infusing my memoir with a depth that I could not have achieved otherwise.

I wholeheartedly embrace the power of place in both my travel writing and memoirs. It is a remarkable force that allows us to connect with history, memories, and personal narratives in ways that words alone cannot capture. By immersing ourselves in these physical spaces, we breathe life into our stories.

I encourage you to seek out your personal landmarks, revisit the scenes of your life's most significant moments, and allow the power of place to guide your pen. You'll be amazed at the richness it brings to your memoir.

3. THE ART OF OPENING UP

In memoir writing, there exists a profound truth that we must confront. Unless we wholeheartedly decide to open up, our most powerful stories will remain hidden, locked away within the recesses of our hearts and minds. It is through the act of embracing vulnerability and fearlessly baring our souls that we unlock the true essence of memoir and first-person narrative. I call it the "art of opening up."

I have come to realize that the beauty of memoir lies not only in the recounting of events and experiences, but in the raw emotions and intimate revelations that accompany them. It is in those moments of unfiltered honesty that we forge a connection with our readers, inviting them into the depths of our being and allowing them to see the world through our eyes.

The decision to open up is not an easy one. It requires a willingness to confront our insecurities and delve into the depths of our emotions. It demands that we strip away the masks we wear and expose the vulnerabilities that make us human. It is a courageous act, for it requires us to confront our own fears of judgment, rejection, and the exposure of our innermost selves.

When we open up, we grant ourselves the freedom to explore the complexities of our experiences, to examine the intricacies of our relationships, and to reflect upon the lessons learned along the way. We create a space where authenticity reigns supreme, unburdened by the need for pretense or conformity. It is within this sacred space that our most profound stories take shape.

By embracing vulnerability, we tap into a wellspring of potential within ourselves. We discover that our most personal struggles, triumphs, and moments of self-discovery hold the power to resonate with others on a profound level. Through our willingness to share, we provide solace to those who may have felt alone in their own experiences and inspire them to embark on their own journeys of self-reflection and growth.

In the art of opening up, we find liberation. We shatter the chains that bind our stories, allowing them to flow freely onto the pages before us. We recognize that it is through our willingness to be vulnerable that our narratives gain depth, authenticity, and the ability to touch the hearts and minds of others.

I hope you embrace the "art of opening up," for within it lies the power to unleash the untold stories that have shaped us. Through our willingness to open up, we give voice to the silenced, shed light on the hidden, and create a tapestry of shared experiences that reverberates through time.

DID YOU KNOW JOHN CHEEVER LIKED COMMERCIALS?

I was captivated one day by the unexpected revelation that Mr. Cheever harbored a fascination for TV commercials. It was a peculiar juxtaposition, the merging of the literary world and the realm of advertising, but it intrigued me nonetheless. I couldn't help but share with him that my father, a devoted Cheever fan, held a prominent position as an advertising executive on Madison Avenue.

To my delight, Cheever's curiosity was piqued, and he began to inquire about my father's involvement in commercials and advertising campaigns. He seemed genuinely interested, as if the world of advertising held a certain allure for him—a glimpse into the cultural zeitgeist and a reflection of the world in which we lived. Cheever expressed that one of his favorite aspects of television was watching the commercials, as he believed they served as a unique form of social commentary.

In his characteristic introspective manner, Cheever contemplated the challenges faced by advertisers in conveying a compelling story within the confines of thirty or sixty seconds. He recognized the inherent difficulty in capturing attention, evoking emotions, and effectively conveying a message within such a limited timeframe. It was a testament to his keen understanding of the complexities of storytelling and the art of communication.

As I entered the world of advertising after college—working as an ad agency copywriter and creative director for many years—Cheever's revelations about commercials resonated with me deeply. It added an additional layer of meaning to my work, reinforcing the notion that storytelling was at the core of our craft. It reminded me that even within the realm of advertising, where the pursuit of selling products often took center stage, there was room for creativity, nuance, and a reflection of the human experience.

Cheever's perspective instilled in me a sense of purpose—a reminder that even in the transient world of commercials, there was an opportunity to touch hearts, provoke thought, and leave a lasting impression. It encouraged me to approach my work with a commitment to crafting narratives that affected people, went beyond mere product promotion, and strived to capture the essence of the human story.

CHAPTER 4

Let's Get Down to Writing

In any memoir workshop, the first thing I do is ask everyone to put together a list of ten significant moments from their lives. Creating this list serves several important purposes. Let's explore why this exercise is valuable.

Triggering Memories: Reflecting on significant moments prompts your memory to recall experiences that might have faded over time. This practice helps unearth buried emotions, details, and anecdotes that are essential for crafting a compelling memoir.

Identifying Key Themes: By listing significant moments, you begin to recognize recurring themes or patterns in your life. These themes can serve as the backbone of your memoir, providing cohesion and a sense of purpose to your storytelling.

Setting Priorities: Compiling a list of significant events will help you prioritize which stories are most important to tell. Not every moment will make it into your memoir, but this exercise allows you to assess the relevance of each event, ensuring that you focus on the most compelling narratives.

Uncovering Emotional Resonance: The significant moments you choose to include in your list are likely the ones that have impacted you emotionally. These are the experiences that have shaped you, influenced your decisions, and continue to affect your life today. By identifying them, you tap into a wellspring of raw emotions that can powerfully infuse your memoir with authenticity and depth.

Creating a Personal Timeline: A list of significant moments forms a personal timeline, marking the milestones and turning points in your life. This timeline serves as a framework for organizing your stories and helps you navigate the chronology of your memoir.

Engaging Readers: Including a variety of significant moments in your memoir engages readers on multiple levels. It allows them to connect with the universal themes of human experience while simultaneously relating to the unique aspects of your own life. The diversity of experience adds richness and breadth to your storytelling.

Sparking Reflection and Insight: As you compile your list, you'll likely find yourself reflecting on the impact these moments have had on your personal growth, values, and worldview. This introspection deepens your understanding of yourself and allows you to share important insights in your memoir, inviting readers to contemplate their own lives in the process.

Discovering Untold Stories: Sometimes, the act of listing significant moments prompts you to remember stories you haven't considered before. These untold stories can add depth and intrigue to your memoir, offering fresh perspectives and surprising revelations.

By putting together a list of ten significant moments in your life, you lay the groundwork for a rich and meaningful memoir. This exercise helps you tap into your memories, emotions, and life experiences, guiding you toward the stories that matter most. Embrace the process, and let these moments shape the narrative tapestry of your memoir, capturing the essence of who you are and how your life has been shaped.

Here are some general categories to think about as you start this first important process.

Birth and Early Childhood: Reflect on your earliest memories, like the place you were born and the experiences that shaped your formative years.

Educational Milestones: Think about key moments in your education, such as starting school, memorable teachers, academic achievements, or challenges you faced along the way.

Family Dynamics: Consider significant family events, relationships, and dynamics that have influenced your life. This could include marriages, divorces, births, deaths, or any pivotal moments that shaped your family's dynamics.

Travel and Adventure: Recall memorable trips, vacations, or adventures that have broadened your horizons, exposed you to new cultures, or sparked personal growth.

Career and Professional Milestones: Reflect on your professional journey, including significant jobs, career changes, promotions, or accomplishments that have shaped your identity and influenced your life path.

Personal Challenges and Triumphs: Think about personal struggles you have faced, such as overcoming adversity, battling an illness, or achieving personal goals.

Relationships and Love: Consider meaningful romantic relationships or friendships that have played a role in your life—positively or negatively—and influenced your personal growth.

Turning Points and Epiphanies: Identify moments of clarity or realizations that led to personal transformation or shifts in your perspective, values, or beliefs.

Loss and Grief: Reflect on experiences of loss, whether it be the death of a loved one, the end of a relationship, or the loss of a dream. These moments often shape us in profound ways.

Life Lessons and Reflections: Consider the wisdom and insights you have gained throughout your life. What are the lessons you have learned? What values or principles do you hold dear?

Now you have a starting point. Whether or not any of this material winds up in your book doesn't matter at this point. These details may lead to other stories and memories that are deeply buried in your subconscious. This process is like mapping out a road trip. You are thinking about where you want to go and why you want to go there. You are considering why certain places might be worth visiting.

Once you've addressed this important first process, you can get into the more practical aspects of storytelling. What will make people want to stop what they're doing and read your words?

CREATING THE "WRITE" ENVIRONMENT

I strongly believe that creating a conducive environment for writing is crucial for unleashing creativity and maintaining focus. The environment we choose to write in plays a significant role in shaping our mindset, emotions, and overall productivity. Whether it's an office, a bedroom, a porch, or a park, each setting offers unique advantages that can contribute to a nurturing and inspiring creative experience.

Let's consider the benefits of an office. An office provides a dedicated space solely for writing, which helps establish a professional mindset. It is a place where we can immerse ourselves in our work, free from distractions and interruptions. Having a well-organized and personalized office with a comfortable chair, a spacious desk, and essential writing tools creates a sense of professionalism and focus. Moreover, an office can be adorned with motivational quotes, artwork, or books that align with our writing goals, reinforcing our commitment to the craft.

On the other hand, a bedroom can also serve as an ideal writing environment. It is a space where we can retreat from the outside world and find solitude. Bedrooms often offer a level of comfort and familiarity that can promote relaxation and creativity. By creating a cozy writing corner within the bedroom—complete with soft lighting, cushions, and perhaps some plants—we can establish a tranquil atmosphere conducive to deep thinking and introspection.

Alternatively, the great outdoors can be a source of inspiration for many writers. A porch or a park allows us to reconnect with nature, breathe in fresh air, and escape the confinement of indoor spaces. The beauty of natural surroundings can stimulate our senses and ignite our imagination. Sitting on a porch swing or a park bench, we can observe the world around us, listen to the sounds of birds chirping or leaves rustling, and let our thoughts wander freely. The serenity and vastness of the outdoors can provide a sense of liberation and tranquility, allowing ideas to flow effortlessly.

Regardless of the specific environment, it is important to consider factors that contribute to a nurturing writing space. Natural lighting, for example, positively affects mood and energy levels. Adequate ventilation and comfortable furniture can boost physical well-being during long writing sessions. Additionally, minimizing distractions such as noise, clutter, and digital devices can enhance focus and productivity.

There are some other things that factor into your writing environment—things that will help you focus your writing process and create realistic expectations.

Gather your tools: Keep all your writing tools—such as your computer or notebook, pens, and pencils—nearby. Ensure you have a reliable internet connection if you need to research.

Eliminate distractions: Remove anything that may distract you, such as your phone or other devices that aren't necessary for writing. You can also use noise-cancelling headphones or listen to instrumental music to help you focus.

Set a routine: Developing good writing habits is essential for new writers.

Set realistic goals: Start with small, achievable goals, such as writing for 10–15 minutes a day, and gradually increase the amount of time you spend writing. This will help you build momentum and develop a regular writing habit.

Schedule regular writing time: Treat your writing like any other appointment or commitment, and schedule regular writing time into your calendar. This will help you make writing a priority and ensure that you have dedicated time to work on your craft.

Practice freewriting: Set a timer for 10–15 minutes and write whatever comes to mind without worrying about grammar or structure. This can help you get into the habit of writing regularly and help you generate new ideas.

Surround yourself with inspiration: Hang motivational quotes, photographs, or artwork that inspires you to keep writing.

Stay organized: Keep your writing space organized and clutter-free to minimize distractions and create a peaceful working environment.

Remember, everyone's ideal writing environment is unique to their personality and preferences. Experiment with different spaces and setups until you find what works best for you.

Creating an environment of sensory isolation can be beneficial for delving into your story and vividly capturing its essence. Here are a few suggestions to help you achieve that:

Find a quiet space: Seek out a tranquil location where you can minimize external disturbances. This could be a dedicated writing room, a secluded corner of a library, or a peaceful outdoor setting.

Eliminate distractions: Identify and eliminate potential distractions in your environment. Silence or turn off your phone, close unnecessary tabs on your computer, and ensure that you have a clean and organized workspace.

Set the mood: Consider what atmosphere helps you focus and relax. Some writers prefer complete silence, while others find instrumental music or ambient sounds helpful. Experiment with different options to discover what works best for you.

Engage your senses: Pay attention to the sensory elements in your surroundings. Lighting, temperature, and scent can all influence your state of mind. Experiment with lighting preferences, adjust the temperature to your comfort, and consider diffusing essential oils or burning candles to incorporate calming scents.

Establish a writing routine: Consistency can aid in entering that meditative state. Set aside dedicated writing times, preferably when you're most alert and focused. Creating a routine signals to your mind that it's time to engage in the writing process.

Practice mindfulness techniques: Incorporate mindfulness exercises into your writing routine to help clear your mind and cultivate a sense of focus. Deep breathing, meditation, or even taking a short walk can help you enter a state of calm and receptivity before writing.

By consciously crafting an environment that promotes concentration and relaxation, you can enhance your ability to access significant memories and write your memoir with clarity.

WRITING GROUPS

I cannot stress enough how crucial a writing group can be in your creative process. Sharing your personal stories and experiences requires a willingness to open up, and a writing group provides the perfect environment for vulnerability and connection.

First and foremost, a writing group offers a supportive community of fellow writers who understand the challenges and triumphs that come with writing. They can become your companions on this literary voyage, offering encouragement, constructive feedback, and a genuine interest in your narrative. As you share your memoir drafts, they will provide valuable insights that help you refine your storytelling techniques, identify gaps in your narrative, and suggest ways to enhance the emotional muscle of your memoir. Their feedback can be instrumental in shaping your work.

A writing group provides accountability and structure to your writing process. Writing a memoir can be a daunting task, and it's easy to get overwhelmed or lose motivation along the way. However, when you're part of a writing group, you have regular meetings or deadlines to meet, which keeps you on track and committed to your writing goals. Group members can provide gentle nudges to keep you accountable and ensure you make progress with your memoir.

In addition to feedback and accountability, a writing group offers a diverse range of perspectives and experiences. Each member brings their own unique background, knowledge, and writing style to the table. This diversity enriches your writing by exposing you to different storytelling techniques, narrative structures, and literary influences. It broadens your horizons as a writer and helps you develop your own voice and style. The collective wisdom and varied viewpoints of the group members can help you discover new perspectives to explore in your memoir and allows you to approach your story from fresh and innovative angles.

Being part of a writing group also provides you with a safe space to experiment, take risks, and receive honest feedback. Writing a memoir often involves delving into deeply personal and sometimes sensitive topics. The support and trust within a writing group allows you to explore these emotional depths without fear of judgment. You can test out different narrative approaches, experiment with unconventional storytelling techniques, and receive feedback that helps you strike the right balance between authenticity and readability.

Ultimately, a writing group becomes your community, your cheerleaders, and your sounding board. Their presence can turn what could be a solitary endeavor into a shared experience filled with camaraderie, growth, and mutual support.

LESSONS FROM JOHN CHEEVER

Here are some things John Cheever taught me.

Write what you know: Cheever told me he believed in drawing inspiration from his own life and experiences. He said, "I can't write about anything else but my own life, my family, my environment, and the people I know." This is a valuable lesson for writers, as it encourages them to draw on their own experiences to create authentic and relatable stories.

Use detail to create vivid images: Cheever was known for his ability to create vivid images through the use of precise detail. By focusing on specific sensory details, he brought his stories to life and created a sense of immersion for his readers. This encourages writers to pay attention to details that will make their stories more engaging and memorable. As an example, look at how Cheever sets the stage early in his classic short story "The Swimmer":

> [This was] at the edge of the Westerhazys' pool.... The pool, fed by an artesian well with a high iron content, was a pale shade of green. It was a fine day. In the west there was a massive stand of cumulus cloud, so like a city seen from a distance—from the bow of an approaching ship—that it might have had a name. Lisbon. Hackensack.[i]

---

i   John Cheever, "The Swimmer," *New Yorker*, July 10, 1964, https://www.newyorker.com/magazine/1964/07/18/the-swimmer.

CHAPTER 5

One Piece at a Time

Writing your story is a deeply personal and introspective process. It's a voyage of self-discovery, a chance to reflect on your experiences, and a means to make sense of the tapestry of your life. Through the act of putting pen to paper or fingertips to keyboard, you'll unravel layers of emotions, memories, and insights that have shaped you into the person you are today.

When it comes to writing your memoir, I want to assure you that you won't be tackling the entire book all at once. Instead, we'll break it down into manageable pieces and take it story by story.

Think of your memoir as a collection of stories. By crafting a solid outline and knowing which stories you want to include, you can take on one little piece at a time. This approach allows you to focus your energy and creativity on each individual story—giving it the attention it deserves—rather than being intimidated by the daunting task of writing a book.

The beauty of this approach is that you can maintain momentum and feel accomplished throughout the writing process. As you complete each story, you'll feel a sense of satisfaction and progress. It's a wonderful feeling to know that you're capturing the essence of your experiences, one narrative at a time.

Breaking it down story by story also gives you the opportunity to explore each one deeply. You can dive into the details, emotions, and reflections that make your memoir truly meaningful, ensuring that every story connects with your readers and conveys the essence of your journey.

Another advantage of this approach is the flexibility it provides. You can choose to work on different stories based on your mood or inspiration. There's no rigid order to follow; you can write what feels right in the moment. This organic flow allows your creativity to flourish and ensures that each story receives the attention it deserves.

Remember, you're not locked into a fixed plan. Revisiting and revising stories is part of the process. You can refine and perfect them over time, ensuring that your memoir is a true reflection of your experiences and insights.

So, don't let the idea of writing your entire memoir overwhelm you. It's not about getting rich or even getting published. In the end, what truly matters is the transformative experience you will embark upon. Take it one story at a time, and you'll find that the process becomes more manageable, enjoyable, and rewarding.

You've got your list of potential stories you've created. We'll start working on those shortly. But let's get to a quick (and, I think, *fun*) assignment to help get you off the ground.

THE SIX-WORD STORY

The six-word story concept begins with Ernest Hemingway, who was known for his concise and impactful writing style. Legend has it that Hemingway was once challenged to write a complete story in just six words. In response, he wrote: "For sale: baby shoes, never worn." This six-word story is said to have encapsulated a heartbreaking tale of loss, evoking powerful emotions in such few words.

Inspired by Hemingway's six-word story, a project called "Six-Word Memoirs" was launched by *SMITH Magazine* in 2006. The idea behind this project was to invite people from all walks of life to share their life stories using only six words. The concept quickly gained popularity, and thousands of people began submitting their own six-word memoirs.

The beauty of the six-word memoir is in its brevity. It's challenging to convey a meaningful story within such a limited space. This exercise encourages people to distill the essence of their experiences, emotions, and identities into a concise format. Six-word memoirs often rely on clever wordplay, juxtaposition, and hints of larger narratives to convey a deeper meaning.

The concept works by inviting individuals to reflect on their lives and distill their experiences into a concise statement. The six-word memoirs can touch upon various aspects of life, including relationships, personal growth, struggles, achievements, and more. The format allows writers to express their unique perspectives, capturing the essence of their lives in a few carefully chosen words.

The six-word memoirs project has expanded into books (most notably *Not Quite What I Was Planning*), online communities, and social media platforms, where people continue to share their own six-word memoirs and engage in discussions about life's complexities. This has become a creative and introspective exercise that demonstrates the power of storytelling and the art of brevity. In my opinion, it's a fun and creative way to

distill a complex or significant experience into a concise statement. One of the first six-word memoirs I wrote was, "Writes
about others, learns about self."

Here are some other examples of six-word memoirs that students in my memoir workshops have shared:

"Embraced challenges, found strength,
wrote story."

"Lost, loved, learned, rose, wrote, conquered."

"Dreamed big, stumbled, persisted,
achieved more."

"Navigated twists, turned pain into power."

"Fell, rose, stumbled, soared, wrote, inspired."

"Wanderlust-filled soul, found home in travel."

"Laughed loudly, loved deeply, lived fully."

"Cherished moments, created memories,
embraced life."

"Savored flavors, cooked love, shared meals."

"Danced through storms, found
sunshine within."

These six-word memoirs are short and powerful, capturing
the essence of a life story or experience in a way that is both
concise and emotionally resonant. It's a great starting point for
what we are about to embark upon. Give it a shot!

JOURNALING

When beginning a personal writing project, journaling can play a crucial role. It serves as a foundational tool that helps authors explore their memories, emotions, and experiences, providing a rich source of material for memoir writing. Journaling not only aids in capturing the essence of personal stories—it facilitates the writing process by enhancing self-reflection, improving writing skills, and maintaining consistency throughout the project.

Journaling allows authors to tap into their memories and experiences, unlocking forgotten details and emotions associated with specific events. By regularly recording thoughts, feelings, and observations, writers can access a wealth of material that may have otherwise been lost or overlooked. These personal reflections can provide valuable insights and anecdotes that contribute to a more comprehensive and authentic memoir.

Writing a memoir often involves revisiting intense or emotionally charged moments from the past. Journaling provides a safe and private space to express and process these emotions. Through journaling, authors can freely explore their feelings, thoughts, and reactions to past events without the pressure of crafting a polished narrative. This emotional catharsis can lead to deeper self-awareness and a more nuanced portrayal of personal experiences in the memoir.

Journaling serves as a practice ground for honing your writing skills. Regularly transcribing thoughts and experiences into words helps authors refine their storytelling abilities, experiment with different writing styles, and develop a unique voice. Journaling also helps authors build discipline and consistency in their writing habits, which is essential for completing a memoir project. As writers become more comfortable expressing themselves through journaling, they gain confidence and proficiency in articulating their memories and stories.

A memoir requires a well-structured narrative that engages readers and maintains coherence. Journaling allows authors to brainstorm ideas, outline potential storylines, and map out the structure of their memoir. By capturing thoughts, themes, and significant events in a journal, authors can identify patterns, connections, and chronological order, which are essential for building a strong narrative arc. Journaling thus becomes a valuable tool for organizing and shaping the memoir's content.

As authors progress with their memoir, they may encounter challenges—such as remembering specific details, timelines, or dialogue. Journaling acts as a reference guide, providing a written record of past experiences that can be revisited when needed. The journal becomes a treasure trove of personal anecdotes, descriptions, and insights, ensuring accuracy in the memoir.

Journaling allows authors to reflect on their personal growth and transformation over time. It provides an opportunity to gain perspective on past events, evaluate decisions made, and understand the impact of those experiences on their lives. By revisiting journal entries, authors can trace the evolution of their thoughts, emotions, and perspectives, enhancing the depth and introspection in their memoir. John Cheever certainly appreciated the power of journaling. His journals were published in 1991, offering fans a remarkable and revealing study of the author himself. Spanning over three decades—beginning with the late 1940s—these journals provide insights into Cheever's personal life, his literary pursuits, and his emotional journey.

Here are some tips to help you get started:

Choose the Right Journal: Find a journal that appeals to you aesthetically and feels comfortable to write in. Whether it's a physical notebook or a digital journaling app, select a format that suits your preferences and encourages you to write regularly.

Set a Regular Writing Schedule: Establish a consistent writing routine that works for you. Determine a specific time of day or allocate a certain number of minutes each day for journaling. Consistency is key to forming a habit and reaping the benefits of journaling.

Write Freely and Authentically: Remember that your journal is a personal and private space. Write without self-censorship or judgment. Allow yourself to freely express your thoughts, emotions, and experiences. Embrace your authentic voice and let your words flow naturally.

Start with Simple Prompts: If you're unsure where to begin, start with simple prompts to kickstart your writing. Consider questions like "How was my day?" or "What am I grateful for today?" These prompts can help you focus your thoughts and initiate the writing process.

Embrace Different Writing Styles: Explore different writing styles and techniques to keep your journaling practice fresh. You can experiment with narrative storytelling, reflective writing, poetry, lists, or even doodling. Don't be afraid to mix it up.

Write for Yourself: Remember that your journal is for your eyes only. Write without worrying about an audience or external judgment. This frees you to be honest and true to yourself in your writing.

Use Journaling as Self-Reflection: Journaling is a powerful tool for self-reflection and personal growth. Take time to reflect on your experiences, emotions, and thoughts. Consider writing about your aspirations, challenges, and lessons learned. Use your journal as a space for introspection and gaining clarity.

Be Consistent and Persistent: Building a journaling habit takes time and commitment. Even if you miss a day or two, don't get discouraged. Just pick up where you left off and continue writing. The more you practice, the more natural and beneficial journaling will become.

Experiment with Different Formats: Journaling doesn't have to be limited to written entries. Explore other creative formats, such as drawing, collages, or incorporating photographs. Mix and match different mediums to make your journaling experience more dynamic and enjoyable.

Review and Reflect: Periodically review your past journal entries. Reflect on the growth, changes, and patterns that occur over time. This reflection can provide valuable insights and serve as a source of inspiration for future writing.

Remember, journaling is personal and there are no hard and fast rules. Adapt these tips to suit your preferences and make your journaling practice an enjoyable and meaningful experience.

Discovering something buried in an old journal can be a magical experience that instantly transports us back in time. As you stumble upon the pages—physically or digitally—memories of the emotions you once felt when writing late at night come rushing back. Maybe the simple act of writing while in bed—pen in hand, letting the words flow onto the spiral notebook paper—brought a sense of fulfillment and contentment.

Today, digital journals offer a compelling alternative to traditional handwritten journals for several reasons. Firstly, they provide unparalleled convenience and accessibility, allowing you to capture your thoughts and experiences anytime, anywhere, using a computer, tablet, or smartphone. Also, digital journals often come with built-in organizational features, such as tags, search functions, and the ability to categorize entries, making it easier to retrieve and reflect on past entries. Digital platforms also frequently offer the option to incorporate multimedia elements, such as photos, videos, and audio recordings, enriching the journaling experience and enabling a more comprehensive documentation of memories. And of course, the digital format provides an added layer of privacy and security, with options for password protection and encryption, ensuring that personal reflections remain confidential.

For me as a teenager, those late-night writing sessions held a unique enchantment. It was a time when the world seemed to quiet down and I could tap into my thoughts and emotions, capturing the essence of something that had just happened. The solitude of the moment allowed my creativity to flourish, unencumbered by distractions or obligations.

There is a raw and genuine quality to penning thoughts onto paper—a tactile connection that enhances the experience. Feeling the weight of the pen, hearing the gentle scratch of its movement across the page… It's as if you are etching your memories and reflections into existence, preserving them for eternity.

In those solitary moments, I was the sole creator of my world, shaping the narrative with each stroke of my pen. Writing became a form of release, a cathartic expression of my innermost thoughts and feelings. It was a space where I could freely explore ideas, grapple with emotions, and make sense of the world around me.

Rediscovering that buried treasure in your journal reminds you of the pure joy that comes from pouring your heart onto the page. It serves as a gentle nudge, an invitation to once again embrace those late-night writing sessions, to reconnect with the magic of self-expression, and to find solace in the act of putting pen to paper. Here's an entry of mine from the summer of 1978:

Journal Entry:

5/23/78 1:30 a.m.

We saw Keith Richards tonight. We were all hunkered down, right across the street from his house in South Salem. It was me, Smitty, Maitland, and McGuire, caught up in the thrill of the chase.

A big, long boat of a car pulled into his driveway… its sleek silhouette suggesting a dark blue Bentley, but it was hard to make out the details. And there he was, behind the wheel, a cigarette glowing in his mouth. We held our breath…

Simultaneously, on the cassette player in the car, we had cranked up an incredible bootleg recording from 1973. Stones live in Rotterdam, and "Gimme Shelter" was blasting through the speakers just as the car pulled up.

As the car door opened, a dark figure emerged. He flicked his cigarette down, stubbing it out with a casual nonchalance. Then, he looked up at the majesty of the full moon, its radiant glow casting a soft white light over the property. It was as if the moon itself acknowledged his presence.

...unmistakably him, he shook his head, muttered something to himself, and made his way towards the front door.

Here's something else to consider: journaling serves as a dynamic companion to the memoir writing process, offering a space for experimentation and discovery. While memoir writing involves the crafting of a cohesive narrative from the vast landscape of one's life, journaling provides a platform for exploration and contemplation. In essence, journaling and memoir writing are distinct yet interconnected processes. Sometimes in workshops, I'll give an assignment that directs writers to take a journal entry and expand on the chosen moment or theme, focusing on creating a structured narrative that includes descriptive details, dialogue, and reflection. It's a good way to let your journal inspire more structured storytelling.

This is a story I wrote based on the circumstances surrounding that journal entry I just shared:

Something happened during the summer of 1979 that still resonates with me today. It was a time when my group of high school senior friends, consisting of about five of us, shared an immense love for the Rolling Stones. We were die-hards, and we made it a tradition to gather outside Keith Richards' house on a beautiful winding country road in South Salem. For us, it became a rite of passage, a place where we felt a special connection to our musical idols.

As we stood there, leaning against the old oak tree that shaded the road, we couldn't help but wonder what was happening inside that grand house. We would let our imaginations run wild, concocting stories of wild parties, jam sessions, and secret recording sessions taking place behind those closed doors. But more than anything, those moments outside Keith's house became our sanctuary, a place where we could share our deepest secrets and personal stories with each other.

We would sit on the grass, forming a tight circle, and begin to open up. The warm summer breeze would carry our words away, as if nature itself was eager to listen to our youthful confessions. One by one, we would reveal our fears, dreams, and hidden desires. We were forming a bond that transcended our shared admiration for the Rolling Stones. But every once in a while, the allure of actually catching a glimpse of the iconic music legend would become too strong to resist. We would gather our courage and concoct elaborate plans to knock on the door, hoping to trick our way into a brief encounter with Keith Richards himself. We would rehearse our lines, trying to sound casual and convincing.

One sunny afternoon, our anticipation reached its peak, and we decided it was time to make our move. Hearts pounding, we approached the massive front door of Keith's house and knocked with a mixture of nerves and excitement. The door creaked open, revealing a middle-aged nanny, her eyes filled with suspicion.

"Can I help you?" she asked, her tone cautious. Stammering, we stumbled over our words, trying to come up with a believable story. But the truth was, we had none. Our plan, hastily put together in the heat of the moment, had crumbled under the weight of our nervousness. We stood there, a group of awkward teenagers, unable to articulate our purpose for being at Keith Richards' doorstep. "Is Keith home?" one of us asked.

The nanny's gaze hardened. "I'm sorry, but I can't help you. You'll have to leave."

Disheartened, we exchanged glances, realizing that our attempt to catch a glimpse of our idol had once again ended in disappointment. We turned away from the door, feeling a mix of embarrassment and resignation.

As we walked back to our familiar spot under the oak tree, we couldn't help but laugh at our failed attempt. The incident only strengthened our resolve to keep returning to that winding country road, gathering outside Keith Richards' house. It wasn't about meeting him anymore; it was about the bond we had forged and the memories we had created in that sacred space.

The summer of 1979 became etched in our hearts as a time of adventure and the pursuit of our musical hero.

As the summer drew to a close and our college plans loomed ahead, we decided to pay one final visit to the house. We approached the door and knocked, but there was no answer. Just as disappointment began to settle in, a young man, about twenty years old, appeared around the corner. He was dressed in a sheepherder's frock, holding a staff above his head, reminiscent of Moses. It was a peculiar sight, but he greeted us with kindness and seemed genuinely willing to help.

We quickly fabricated a story, claiming that our car had overheated. Without hesitation, the young man assured us it was not a problem. Moments later, he returned with a jug of water, ready to assist us. However, as we looked into his eyes, a sense of honesty compelled us to confess the real reason for our visit. We asked him if Keith was home, hoping for a glimmer of confirmation that our idol might be within those walls.

The young man's expression turned serious, and he gently explained that Keith was not at home and that our actions would not be appreciated. It was as if he carried a wisdom beyond his years. His words struck a chord deep within us, awakening a profound realization. We understood that it was time to let go of our fantasies and move forward with our lives. It was an epiphany, a turning point that we needed.

Days later, as we perused the pages of a small local newspaper, a shocking headline caught our attention. The story reported the tragic death of a seventeen-year-old boy named Scott Cantrell. Supposed suicide. A single pistol shot to the skull while lying in Keith Richard's bed. It struck us with a shocking jolt of recognition—the young man we had encountered in front of Keith

Richards' house. Scott, a young drifter, had somehow found his way to the house one fateful day. There, he became entangled with Anita Pallenberg, the once-glamorous model and Keith's wife. Anita's struggles with heroin addiction were well-known, and it seemed that Scott had been drawn into that dangerous world.

The house, which had once held so much allure for us, now revealed itself as a place that had taken Scott's life. The news of Scott's death shook us to the core. It was shocking, to say the least, to learn that he was just seventeen years old, the same age as us back then. As we delved deeper into the details, a dark and tragic story unfolded before our eyes. The news of Scott's death sent shockwaves through the small bucolic community of South Salem. It was a tranquil place, far removed from the darker undercurrents of the music industry. The tragedy disrupted the peaceful facade, forcing us to confront the harsh realities that could lurk beneath the surface.

As the weight of the revelation sank in, we were left speechless. Our encounter with Scott, as strange and fleeting as it was, had left an indelible mark on us. In his own way, he had offered us guidance and closure. It was a bittersweet realization that life is fragile, and the paths we choose can lead to unforeseen consequences.

Scott's untimely death served as a poignant reminder that we needed to embrace the present and pursue our own dreams. We carried his memory with us as we embarked on our separate journeys, forever changed by that summer of camaraderie, secrets shared, and the unexpected encounter that forced us to confront the transient nature of life.

For me, personally, it was a profound awakening. It shattered the innocence and idealism I had associated with the band I loved most, The Rolling Stones. It took time to process the weight of that harsh reality. The experience exposed us to the dark side, the dangers that could come with idolizing and worshiping our musical heroes.

It made us realize that there were aspects of their lives we didn't know about, hidden shadows that could affect how we listened to their music. It was a sobering lesson in the complexities of fame, addiction, and the consequences that could arise from being too close to the flame.

As time went on, we carried the memory of Scott's tragic fate with us. It served as a cautionary tale, a reminder to approach our passions with a measure of caution and to be aware of the complexities that lie beneath the surface. It didn't diminish our love for The Rolling Stones or music in general, but it added a layer of maturity and skepticism to our appreciation.

In the end, our time outside Keith Richards' house became a defining chapter in our lives, a testament to the power of music, friendship, and the profound impact of chance encounters. And as we moved on, we held onto the lessons learned, forever grateful for the role that summer played in shaping who we would become.

THE "V" WORD: VULNERABILITY

First and foremost, vulnerability allows for a deep and genuine connection with your readers. By sharing your struggles and triumphs, you invite readers into your world on a profoundly emotional level. They can relate to your experiences, empathize with you, and find solace, inspiration, or resonance in your story. When you're willing to be vulnerable, you create an authentic and heartfelt connection with your readers. This connection makes your memoir a truly impactful and meaningful piece of writing.

Embracing vulnerability in your memoir also allows for emotional honesty and truthfulness. By opening up about your fears, insecurities, and moments of weakness, you paint a realistic and relatable picture of your life. Readers appreciate and respect the courage it takes to confront and share these vulnerabilities. They are more likely to trust and engage with your narrative once they see your willingness to be honest and transparent.

Vulnerability fosters personal growth and healing. By confronting and articulating your vulnerabilities, you gain a deeper understanding of yourself and your experiences. This process of introspection can be transformative, allowing you to make sense of your past, find closure, and even uncover healing.

I understand that vulnerability can be scary. It requires you to confront past traumas, insecurities, and moments of weakness head-on. However, it is precisely in this vulnerability that the power of your memoir lies. It is through vulnerability that you create space for empathy, connection, and understanding. Remember that you are not alone in this process. Writing communities, supportive friends, or even therapy can provide a safe space for you to explore and process these emotions as you write your memoir.

Ultimately, effective writing requires a willingness to be vulnerable. That's how you forge a deep connection with your readers. So, embrace these feelings and acknowledge that they are an integral part of your story. Trust in the power of vulnerability and you will find that your memoir becomes a compelling and transformative piece of writing that resonates with audiences far and wide.

Here are a several examples of vulnerabilities that can be explored:

Loss and Grief: Share the experience of losing a loved one and the emotional mark it left on your life. Explore the raw emotions, the stages of grief, and the process of healing.

Mental Health Struggles: Open up about your personal battles with anxiety, depression, or other mental health issues. Discuss the challenges faced, seeking help, and finding coping mechanisms.

Identity and Self-Discovery: Explore questions of race, gender, sexuality, or cultural heritage. Sharing the path of self-discovery, acceptance, and finding one's true self.

Addiction and Recovery: Share moments of addiction, what it did to your life and relationships, and the journey of recovery. Discuss the struggles, setbacks, and triumphs along the path to sobriety.

Trauma and Healing: Address traumatic events from the past and their lasting effects. Share the process of healing, seeking therapy, and finding ways to move forward while acknowledging what the trauma did to you.

Family Dynamics: Explore issues with family relationships, such as estrangement, divorce, or dysfunction. Reflect on the complexities of these dynamics, the emotional toll, and the path toward forgiveness or reconciliation.

Self-Doubt and Insecurities: Share moments of self-doubt, imposter syndrome, or feelings of inadequacy.

These are just a few examples, and they can vary widely depending on individual experiences and stories. The key is to delve into the emotions, challenges, and transformative moments that have shaped your life, and to share them with honesty. Remember, it is in these vulnerable moments that your memoir becomes relatable, impactful, and deeply resonant with readers.

A JOHN CHEEVER MEMORY

I never felt the need to share with my friends that I was visiting John Cheever. It somehow didn't fit into our regular conversations or activities. Perhaps he didn't seem "cool" in the way that teenage minds perceive coolness. Nevertheless, when my high school English teacher found out about my friendship with John Cheever, he was utterly flabbergasted. "You actually know John Cheever?" he exclaimed, his eyes wide with disbelief. At the time, I didn't fully grasp the magnitude of the situation or comprehend what a big deal it was to have a personal connection to such a celebrated writer.

That is, until one day—while accompanying my mother to the supermarket, I stumbled upon a magazine rack at the checkout. As I glanced up, I saw John Cheever's face staring back at me from the cover of *Newsweek*. I couldn't believe my eyes. I knew this guy! I quickly purchased the magazine, eager to explore the article featuring the man who had become a mentor to me.

Arriving at Cheever's house later that day, I couldn't help but express my astonishment. "I have to be honest, Mr. Cheever," I confessed. "I didn't know you were this big." I wondered aloud why he even allowed me into his world. In response, he kindly and sincerely explained that when I had first written to him, he was in the midst of rebuilding his life, including repairing his relationship with his wife. He admitted that he had been struggling with alcoholism, describing himself as a "drunken mess." He went on to say that receiving my letter gave him a small chance to help someone else and, in turn, bring some clarity to his own life.

In that moment, the magnitude of his gesture truly sank in. I realized that my presence in his life, however insignificant it may have seemed to me, had provided him with a sense of purpose and the opportunity to offer guidance to a young aspiring writer. It was a reminder that even the most accomplished individuals face their own battles and seek solace and meaning through connections with others.

Looking back, I wish I had fully understood the significance of my interactions with John Cheever during my teenage years. It was a remarkable privilege to have had the chance to learn from him. His willingness to share his wisdom and mentorship with me—despite his personal struggles—remains a treasured memory that continues to inspire me.

Then again, maybe it's better that I didn't fully understand the gift he had given me. Perhaps I would've acted differently or brought undue attention to it. Maybe it played out just as it was meant to be.

CHAPTER 6

The Most Essential Elements

To make your memoir engaging, several vital components need to be considered: showing rather than telling, sensory writing, and defining your voice. These elements work together to create an immersive reading experience, allowing readers to connect with the author's story on a deeper level.

SHOW, DON'T TELL

Rather than simply stating facts or emotions, authors should strive to reveal these details through strong descriptions, concrete details, and compelling anecdotes. By painting a vibrant picture with words, authors can engage readers' senses and allow them to experience the events and emotions themselves. This technique helps the audience feel connected to the author's story and creates a more compelling reading experience.

The "show, don't tell" concept is credited to Russian playwright Anton Chekhov, who allegedly said, "Don't tell me the moon is shining; show me the glint of light on broken glass." (Chekhov actually said, in a letter to his brother, "In descriptions of Nature one must seize on small details, grouping them so that when the reader closes his eyes he gets a picture. For instance, you'll have a moonlit night if you write that on the mill dam a piece of glass from a broken bottle glittered like a bright little star, and that the black shadow of a dog or a wolf rolled past like a ball.")

You get the idea. That said, it was Ernest Hemingway who truly helped popularize this seemingly elusive technique. He was known for his minimalist writing style that was characterized by sparse prose, concise descriptions, and a focus on action and dialogue rather than introspection or lengthy explanations. Hemingway believed in allowing readers to draw their own conclusions; he wanted them to experience the story through the actions and behavior of the characters, rather than explicitly telling them what to think or feel. He favored concrete details, sensory imagery, and understatement to convey meaning and emotions.

By employing this approach, Hemingway aimed to create a sense of immediacy and realism in his works. He trusted his audience to infer deeper meanings and emotions from the surface-level events and interactions that he presented.

SENSORY WRITING

Sensory writing is closely related to "show, don't tell," and involves appealing to the reader's senses. By incorporating sensory details—such as sights, sounds, smells, tastes, and textures—authors can bring their experiences to life on the page. Sensory writing adds depth and richness to the narrative, allowing readers to fully immerse themselves in the author's world. Whether it's describing the aroma of a home-cooked meal or the feeling of the wind on their face, these sensory details help the audience connect with the story on an emotional level.

DEFINING YOUR VOICE

Your voice reflects your unique personality, perspective, and style as an author. It encompasses the tone, language, and over-all narrative style that you employ throughout your memoir. Developing a strong and authentic voice helps readers connect with you as a person and understand your experiences more intimately. Finding your distinct voice allows your story to shine through and distinguish your memoir from others.

When combined, these elements create a powerful and compelling memoir that impacts readers. Showing and not tell-ing engages readers' imaginations and allows them to experience the story alongside the author. Sensory writing brings the nar-rative to life by appealing to readers' senses, making the story more tangible and relatable. Defining your voice establishes a personal connection between the author and the reader, foster-ing empathy and understanding.

Now let's break down each of these elements.

SHOW, DON'T TELL

If you take one thing away from this book, I hope this is it. This device is the foundation, the approach that makes the reader feel as if they are right there with you (which is what you want). "Show, don't tell" is common writing advice, particularly in cre-ative writing. It means that, instead of telling the reader what is happening or how a character feels, the writer should use sen-sory details, actions, and dialogue to create a strong image. This allows the reader to experience the story for themselves.

For example, instead of writing "John was angry," the writer could show John slamming the door, clenching his fists, and shouting at the top of his lungs. By using sensory details and actions, the writer allows people to infer that John is angry, rather than simply telling them.

Showing, rather than telling, helps create a more immersive reading experience. Through this approach, the reader is able to feel the story for themselves and draw their own conclusions. It also allows for a deeper understanding of characters and their motivations, as their actions and behaviors reveal more about their personality and emotions than simply describing them could.

Instead of stating a place is beautiful, describe what makes it beautiful. For example, "The sun dipped below the horizon, painting the sky with streaks of pink and orange. The trees swayed gently in the breeze, their leaves rustling like whispers."

Instead of writing that a character is nervous, show their nervousness through physical descriptions and internal thoughts. For example, "She twisted her hands together, her palms slick with sweat. *What if I mess this up?* she thought, her heart racing."

Instead of telling us that a character is in love, show the love through their actions and dialogue. For example, "He reached for her hand, his fingers lacing with hers. 'I love you,' he whispered, his eyes soft and warm."

Instead of stating a character is brave, show their bravery through their response to a challenging situation. For example, "She stood her ground, facing the bull with steady eyes and a calm demeanor. She didn't flinch as it charged toward her, holding her ground until the last possible moment."

Instead of "I was scared," show the fear: "My heart raced as I heard the creaking floorboards and imagined the worst. I took deep breaths, trying to steady my shaking hands, and tried to think of a way out."

Why say "I loved my grandmother" when you can show the love instead: "My grandmother's warm, wrinkled hand engulfed mine as we strolled through the park. She pointed out each flower and bird, and I felt a surge of love for this kind and gentle woman who had always been there for me."

Instead of, "The party was fun," show the atmosphere: "The room was alive with music and laughter, and the air was thick with the scent of warm food and wine. I danced with abandon, feeling the beat of the music pulse through my veins, and lost myself in the joy of the moment."

When showing instead of telling, a description like "He was angry" becomes "His face turned red, and his eyes narrowed as he glared at me. His voice rose in anger, and his fists clenched at his sides. I took a step back, suddenly feeling the weight of his rage."

In each of these examples, the author is using descriptive language and sensory details to show what is happening and how the narrator is feeling, rather than simply stating an emotion. This approach can help the reader connect more deeply with the narrator's experiences and emotions.

SENSORY WRITING

When writing with your senses, use descriptive language to create a true sensory experience for your reader. This means engaging with your surroundings and using sensory details to describe what you see, hear, smell, taste, and feel. Writing with your senses is a powerful way to bring your perspective to life, as it helps your readers feel fully immersed in your story.

Here are some tips for writing with your senses:

Engage all five senses: Use descriptive language to bring the sights, sounds, smells, tastes, and sensations of your surroundings to life.

Use strong verbs: Strong, active verbs help create a sense of movement and action, allowing your reader to feel fully immersed in the scene.

Use concrete details: Specific, concrete details help ground your writing in reality, making it more relatable to your reader.

Be specific: Rather than using general terms, be as specific as possible in your descriptions. For example, instead of saying "the food smelled good," describe the specific aromas and flavors that make up the dish.

Use figurative language: Metaphors, similes, and other forms of figurative language can help create memorable images in a reader's mind. (A metaphor is a figure of speech that directly compares two unrelated things by stating that one thing is another. For example, "The world is a stage." A simile is a figure of speech that compares two different things using "like" or "as." For example, "Her eyes sparkled like diamonds.") Both metaphors and similes are used to make descriptions more vivid and to convey abstract ideas in a more tangible way.

Sensory writing can help bring a memoir to life and create a more visceral experience for the reader. Here are some examples of sensory writing for a memoir:

Sight: Use descriptive language to paint a picture. For example:

> "The sun was setting, casting a golden light over the trees. The leaves rustled in the breeze, their colors ranging from deep red to vibrant yellow."

> "The city skyline stretched out before me, with towering skyscrapers reaching up to the sky."

> "The leaves on the trees glowed like fiery jewels in the autumn sun."

> "The storm clouds gathered on the horizon, dark and ominous, like a warning of things to come."

> "The crowded market was a riot of colors and textures, with bright fruits and vegetables piled high on the stalls."

> "The stars twinkled in the clear night sky like a thousand tiny lights, illuminating the darkness."

Sound: Use sounds to create a sense of atmosphere. For example:

> "The roar of the waves crashing against the shore was deafening. The seagulls screeched overhead, their cries piercing through the sound of the water."

"The rain pattered against the roof, a soothing rhythm that lulled me to sleep."

"The silence in the room was so thick you could hear a pin drop."

"The wind howled through the trees, a mournful sound that seemed to echo with loneliness."

"The sound of laughter filled the air, a joyous chorus that lifted my spirits."

"The music played softly in the background, a gentle melody that wrapped around me like a warm blanket."

"The crunch of leaves underfoot was a satisfying sound, announcing the arrival of autumn."

Smell: Use smells to evoke memories and emotions. For example:

"The scent of freshly baked bread wafted through the air, bringing back memories of my grandmother's kitchen."

"The smell of saltwater and seaweed reminded me of lazy days spent at the beach as a child."

"The musty smell of old books filled the library, transporting me back to my days as a student."

"The pungent aroma of spices and curry hung in the air, a reminder of my travels to India."

"The sweet, floral scent of honeysuckle filled the garden, a harbinger of summer days to come."

"The sharp tang of chlorine reminded me of long afternoons spent at the pool as a teenager."

Taste: Use taste to create a sense of intimacy and connection. For example:

"The warm, buttery croissant melted in my mouth, delivering me back to a sidewalk cafe in Paris."

"The tangy sweetness of the strawberry jam brought back memories of my mother's home-made preserves."

"The rich, velvety chocolate melted in my mouth, filling me with warmth and happiness."

"The tangy, spicy flavors of the street food in Thailand awakened my senses and left me craving more."

"The sweet, syrupy taste of maple syrup on pancakes reminded me of lazy Sunday mornings with my family."

"The salty, savory flavor of bacon sizzling in the pan made my mouth water and my stomach growl."

"The sharp, tangy taste of fresh citrus awakened my taste buds and filled me with energy."

"The comforting warmth of a steaming cup of tea filled me with a sense of calm and peace."

"The creamy, indulgent flavor of ice cream on a hot summer day was pure bliss."

Touch: Use tactile sensations to create a sense of physicality and emotion. For example:

"The rough bark of the tree scraped against my back as I leaned against it, grounding me in the moment."

"The soft, fluffy fur of my childhood pet rabbit brought me comfort and joy."

"The cool, smooth surface of the pebble in my palm reminded me of the tranquility of nature."

"The hot, steamy water of the shower washed away my stress and left me feeling refreshed."

"The gritty texture of sand between my toes reminded me of the carefree days of childhood summers."

"The soft, plush fabric of my favorite childhood toy brought me comfort and security."

"The warm, enveloping embrace of a loved one made me feel safe and loved."

By using sensory writing, you can transport the reader to the time and place of your memoir and create a more personal, engaged experience.

Here are a few writing exercises for you that incorporate sensory writing and showing rather than telling:

Sensory Details: Write a scene from your memoir using sensory details to convey emotions or experiences. Instead of telling us how you felt, show it through the senses. For example, instead of saying "I was scared," describe the pounding of your heart, the sweatiness of your palms, and the chills running down your spine.

Dialogue: Recreate a conversation from a significant moment in your memoir. Focus on capturing the tone, emotions, and subtext through the characters' words and interactions. Show the dynamics between the people involved without explicitly explaining their relationships or feelings.

Symbolism: Choose an object or symbol that holds meaning in your memoir and use it to show a particular theme or emotion. Instead of stating the theme outright, explore how the object is used, how it appears, and how it's significant within the story.

Action and Body Language: Write a scene where you express a character's emotions or thoughts through their actions and body language. Show their nervousness, excitement, or sadness through gestures, movements, and reactions. This allows readers to interpret the character's state of mind without the author explicitly telling them.

Setting Descriptions: Select a significant location from your memoir and describe it in detail. Use descriptive language to evoke a sense of place, time, and atmosphere. Show the reader how the setting influenced your experiences or shaped your memories.

Remember, the goal of these exercises is to engage readers' senses and imagination, allowing them to experience your memoir firsthand rather than being told about it. By using descriptive language, dialogue, symbolism, and actions, you can create a more immersive narrative.

Hint: Another great assignment to practice showing and not telling—while also incorporating sensory writing—is to describe a meal. Food inherently engages nearly all five senses, making it an ideal subject for exploring descriptive writing in memoirs. Instead of simply stating what the meal consisted of or how it tasted, aim to place your reader into the scene by painting a rich sensory picture.

Example: Stepping into the dim sum restaurant, I was immediately enveloped in an atmosphere buzzing with energy. The aroma of steamed delicacies and the clatter of plates and teacups filled the air, promising a feast for the senses.

The bustling dining hall was a vibrant tapestry of colors and movement. Servers weaved through the crowd, pushing steaming carts laden with bamboo baskets. Each basket held a tantalizing glimpse of its contents, revealing delicate folds of translucent dumpling wrappers, vibrant greens of vegetable-filled parcels, and golden-hued pastries. The sight of these bite-sized treasures made my mouth water in anticipation.

The air was alive with a medley of fragrances that danced playfully around me. The aroma of freshly brewed tea mingled with the earthy scent of steamed rice and the delicate sweetness of lotus leaf-wrapped sticky rice. The faint hint of garlic and the unmistakable tang of soy sauce lingered, adding depth to the olfactory experience. With every breath, my senses were further awakened to the feast that awaited me.

As the carts rolled by, I eagerly selected bamboo baskets, each one holding a unique flavor adventure. I bit into a plump shrimp dumpling, and the tender morsel burst with the briny sweetness of the sea. The velvety texture of the har gow wrapper gave way to the succulent filling, leaving an exquisite taste lingering on my palate. The rich umami of the char siu bao—with its fluffy, golden exterior and sweet barbecue pork filling—melted in my mouth, leaving me craving more.

The act of eating dim sum was a tactile delight. As I picked up a steamed bao, its pillowy softness yielded under my fingers, releasing a fragrant steam. The delicate dumpling skins clung gently to my chopsticks, their tender texture a testament to the skilled hands that crafted them. Each bite brought a satisfying resistance, a delightful interplay between the smoothness of the fillings and the slight chew of the wrappers.

Amidst the lively chatter of diners and the clinking of tea cups, the sounds of dim sum preparation added a rhythmic harmony to the ambiance. The sizzle of dumplings hitting hot pans, the gentle hiss of steam escaping from bamboo steamers, and the occasional clatter of plates being stacked created a symphony of culinary craftsmanship. These sounds became the soundtrack to the shared experience of indulging in this culinary tradition.

WHAT IS YOUR VOICE?

A literary voice refers to the unique writing style or perspective that an author uses in their work to convey ideas, emotions, and themes. It encompasses an author's distinctive use of language, tone, syntax, and other elements of writing that make their work recognizable and unique. The literary voice is what distinguishes one author's work from another, and it is often shaped by the author's background, experiences, and personal beliefs. A strong literary voice can captivate readers and create a lasting impact on their understanding of a particular subject or theme. In short, literary voice is the way an author writes and communicates their message, and it is a crucial element in creating a memorable work of literature.

Literary voice can take many different forms, as every author has their own unique way of expressing themselves. Here are a few examples of different types of literary voice:

Ernest Hemingway: Hemingway's writing style is known for its simplicity, clarity, and directness. He often used short, simple sentences and avoided elaborate descriptions or adjectives, which gave his writing a distinctive voice that was both powerful and understated.

Toni Morrison: Morrison's writing style is characterized by its poetic language and strong imagery. She often explores themes of race, identity, and memory in her work, and her prose is known for its emotional depth and complexity.

J. D. Salinger: Salinger's writing style is marked by its distinctive use of colloquial language. He often wrote in the first person and used a conversational tone that made his characters feel relatable and authentic.

Gabriel García Márquez: Márquez's writing style is known for its magical realism, which blends fantastical elements with real-world events and settings. He often used lush descriptions and intricate metaphors to create a dreamlike atmosphere in his work.

Virginia Woolf: Woolf's writing style is characterized by its stream-of-consciousness narrative technique, which follows the flow of her characters' thoughts and emotions as they unfold in real time. She often used poetic language to create a sense of introspection and interiority in her work.

Your first-person storytelling should reflect your unique perspective and voice. Don't try to emulate another writer or hide behind a persona. Discovering your voice when writing a memoir can be a challenging process, but there are tips below to help you find your unique style and perspective:

Read widely: Read memoirs by a variety of authors to get a sense of different writing styles and voices. Pay attention to how authors convey their experiences and emotions and how they use language to create a particular tone or mood.

Reflect on your experiences: Spend time reflecting on your life experiences and how they have shaped you as a person. Think about what themes and ideas you want to explore in your memoir and how you can convey them in a compelling way.

Write from the heart: Writing a memoir requires honesty. Don't be afraid to write about difficult or painful experiences, and be willing to share your emotions and feelings with your readers.

Seek feedback: Share your writing with others and ask for feedback on your style and voice. Consider joining a writing group or taking a writing workshop to receive additional support and feedback.

Remember that finding your voice takes time and practice, so be patient and keep writing. With persistence and dedication, you can develop a unique and compelling voice. Your voice is the attitude behind your writing—think of it like that.

Here are some writing prompts that can help you define your voice:

Write a letter to your younger self, offering advice or insights based on your life experiences. Use your unique voice to convey wisdom, empathy, and understanding.

Describe a significant event or moment from your life through the lens of a specific emotion, such as joy, anger, fear, or love. Explore how your voice changes when expressing different emotions.

Imagine you're having a conversation with a close friend or family member about a pivotal moment in your life. Write dialogue that captures the authenticity of your voice and the intimacy of the conversation.

Choose a person who has had a major impact on your life. Write a character sketch or a tribute to that person, using your voice to convey the depth of your connection and the emotions that person evokes.

Reflect on a place that holds deep meaning for you—like a childhood home, a favorite vacation spot, or a significant landmark. Write a descriptive passage that captures the essence of that place using your unique voice.

Write a short memoir piece reflecting on a life lesson you have learned. Use your voice to convey the insights, reflections, and personal growth that have resulted from that experience.

Recall a humorous or embarrassing moment from your life. Write a scene that captures the humor or the embarrassment, using your voice to convey the tone and the unique perspective you bring to the situation.

Think about a strong belief or value that has shaped your life. Write a persuasive piece, using your voice to articulate and defend that belief while incorporating personal anecdotes and experiences.

Remember, finding your voice is an ongoing process, and that process may evolve and change over time. These prompts are designed to help you explore different aspects of your voice and bring out your unique perspective and storytelling style.

WORKING WITH THE DOOBIE BROTHERS

Working with Tom Johnston and Pat Simmons—the founders of The Doobie Brothers—on their memoir was an incredibly interesting process. The stark contrast between their personalities and musical styles made the collaboration a unique and fulfilling experience. Tom was a gritty, hard-driving rock 'n' roller, while Pat embodied the folksy essence of a Bay Area bohemian. Together, their distinct voices created the magical chemistry that defined The Doobie Brothers. However, capturing both perspectives in a memoir presented its own set of challenges.

One of the most crucial aspects we discovered while writing the book was the need to balance the different voices and perspectives of Tom and Pat. Finding that balance was essential to ensure that each of them had their own space to express their version of events, even if they didn't always align with one another. The three of us understood the importance of respecting their individual truths based on how they experienced specific stories and moments.

Incorporating multiple points of view required careful navigation. We aimed to present each perspective authentically, even when recounting similar episodes. By doing so, we allowed readers to gain a deeper understanding of the band's dynamics and the unique lens through which each founder viewed their shared experiences.

Throughout the writing process, I encouraged Tom and Pat to share their personal insights and memories, even if they differed from one another. This approach allowed us to capture the essence of their individual experiences and the diverse influences that shaped the Doobie Brothers' music. It was fascinating to witness how their contrasting perspectives complemented each other, creating a more comprehensive and layered narrative.

In the end, the memoir became a testament to the power of embracing two distinct voices. The book showcased the beauty and complexity of collaboration, highlighting the magic that arises when different talents and personalities come together. By respecting and honoring each founder's truth, we were able to create a memoir that celebrated the band's legacy while providing the audience with a deeper connection to the music and the individuals behind it.

CHAPTER 7

How to Tell a Story

Now, I want to start breaking down *how* to tell a story. You can begin by taking some examples from the list of important "story-starter" memories that you made earlier in this book and building them out as stories. But please, before we proceed, never hesitate to go back and revisit the three concepts discussed in the previous chapter. They are integral to any serious writing process.

PYRAMID

Gustav Freytag was a German novelist and playwright who lived from 1816 to 1895. While he is primarily known for his works of fiction, such as his novel *Debit and Credit* (*Soll und Haben*), Freytag also made significant contributions to literary theory.

Freytag's most notable contribution to literary theory is his model of dramatic structure, known as "Freytag's Pyramid" or "Freytag's Five-Act Structure." He outlined this model in his book *The Technique of the Drama* (*Die Technik des Dramas*) published in 1863. Freytag believed that a well-constructed play or narrative should follow a specific pattern of rising action, climax, and falling action, leading to a resolution.

Freytag's Pyramid consists of five parts:

1. Exposition: The beginning of the story, in which the characters, setting, and conflict are introduced. In memoir, exposition can refer to any information that the author provides to help others understand the events and experiences being described. This can include information about the author's family background, cultural context, historical events, or other relevant details.

Exposition helps the reader understand the author's experiences and how they fit into a larger context. For example, if the memoir is about the author's experiences growing up in a particular community, the author may need to provide some exposition about the community's history, cultural norms, and social dynamics to help the reader fully understand the author's experiences. However, it is important for memoir writers to be judicious in their use of exposition. Too much exposition can bog down the narrative and detract from the immediacy and emotional impact of the author's experiences. It is often more effective to provide exposition gradually throughout the memoir, as certain details become relevant to the story being told.

2. Rising action: The part of the story where the conflict becomes more complicated and the tension builds.

Rising action is a literary term that refers to the series of events in a story that build tension. In memoir, rising action can be used to describe events or experiences that lead the author to a significant moment of change or realization—often known as the climax or turning point of the narrative.

For example, in a memoir about overcoming addiction, the rising action might include the author's initial struggles with substance abuse, their failed attempts at sobriety, and their eventual decision to seek treatment. These events build tension and create a sense of anticipation for the climax of the story, which might be the author's successful completion of treatment and their newfound sobriety.

3. Climax: The turning point of the story, where the conflict reaches its highest point and the outcome is decided.

For example, in a memoir about surviving a traumatic event, the climax might be the moment when the author finally confronts and overcomes the emotional or physical aftermath of the event. This might involve a realization or decision that allows the author to move forward with their life in a new and positive direction.

In another memoir, the climax might be a moment of self-discovery or personal growth. For instance, the author might realize the true nature of their feelings for someone or come to a deeper understanding of their own values and beliefs.

The climax is often the most emotionally charged moment in the story and can serve to tie together the various themes and threads of the narrative. By building tension and anticipation throughout the rising action, the climax provides a satisfying and meaningful resolution to the story being told.

4. Descending action: The part of the story where the tension begins to decrease, and the characters respond to the climax.

During the descending action, the author may reflect on the lessons they have learned, the ways in which they have changed or grown, and the impact that their experiences have had on their life. They may also describe how their relationships with other people have evolved, and how they have come to terms with the conflicts or struggles that they've faced.

For example, in a memoir about overcoming addiction, the descending action might involve the author's continued commitment to sobriety, as well as their efforts to repair any damage that their addiction may have caused in their personal life. The author might reflect on the lessons they have learned about addiction, recovery, and personal responsibility, and describe how these lessons will continue to shape their life moving forward.

Descending action is important because it provides closure to the story and helps the audience understand the broader significance of the events and experiences being described. It also allows the author to reflect on their journey and to contemplate how this change will impact their lives.

5. Denouement/Resolution: The end of the story, in which the conflict is resolved and the characters' lives return to a new normal.

In memoir, denouement often involves the author reflecting on their experiences and the impact they've had on their life. This reflection can take many forms, including a summary of the lessons that the author has learned, an assessment of how their experiences have shaped their worldview or identity, or a discussion of how they plan to move forward with their life.

For example, in a memoir about overcoming a serious illness, the denouement might involve the author reflecting on their path to recovery and the lessons they've learned about their own strength and resilience. They might describe how their experiences have given them a new perspective on life and how they plan to move forward with gratitude and a renewed sense of purpose.

Denouement is an important part of memoir writing, because it provides closure to the audience and helps tie together the various themes and threads of the narrative. It allows the author to reflect on the events that occurred and to provide a sense of resolution and meaning to the story being told, leaving the reader with a lasting impression of the author's experiences and insights.

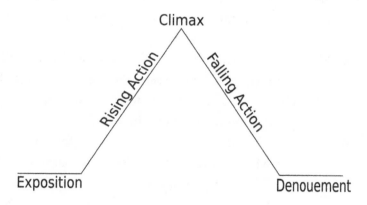

There you have it! I've used Freytag's Pyramid in writing workshops since I started doing them almost ten years ago. It's a useful tool for analyzing and understanding the structure of a story, as well as identifying the key moments of tension and conflict, then figuring out how they are resolved. It is also a helpful guide for memoir writers, as it can be used to plan and structure their stories, ensuring that they have a clear beginning, middle, and end, and that the tension builds and resolves in a satisfying way.

Right before the pandemic started in 2020, I was starting a new memoir workshop. Just a day or two before the first session, we had to put our beloved dog, Marilyn, down. I was obviously still very upset when the workshop started because Marilyn was on my mind (she still is). I decided to use the memory as a way to illustrate the five parts of the pyramid:

1. I've always loved dogs and fifteen years ago, we went looking for the perfect addition to our family.
2. Marilyn was the sweetest animal I'd ever met and when we adopted her, she became an integral part of our lives; an essential member of our family. Since I work from home, she became my shadow, companion, and one of the best friends I've ever had.
3. She began growing ill in the last year, and her quality of life severely declined. Several days ago, we made the hard choice to have her put down. It was one of the most painful moments of my life.
4. Home is not the same anymore, at least for now. I see and hear Marilyn everywhere. I sense her around each corner and in every room, and I miss her terribly.
5. Having Marilyn taught me about devotion, loyalty, and unconditional love. The hole she has left in my heart is

evidence not of loss, but rather a deep and abiding love and affection.

It's basic, of course, but this gives me an outline—should I ever want to write something more long form about Marilyn or about my love of dogs and how they have affected and shaped my life. That's what so many of these little exercises do: they give you a working outline that prepares you for the heavy lifting.

Here are a few more examples. Let's consider the classic fairytale *Cinderella*:

1. **Exposition**: The story begins by introducing Cinderella, a young girl who lives with her evil stepmother and stepsisters.

2. **Rising Action**: In *Cinderella*, the rising action includes Cinderella's daily struggles and her desire to attend the royal ball, the introduction of the Fairy Godmother, and the transformation of Cinderella into a beautiful princess.

3. **Climax**: The climax occurs when Cinderella arrives at the ball and captures the attention of the prince. The moment of truth is when the prince recognizes Cinderella as his true love.

4. **Falling Action**: The falling action includes the prince searching for Cinderella and fitting the glass slipper on her foot. It also involves the confrontation between Cinderella and her stepmother and stepsisters.

5. **Resolution**: The resolution occurs when Cinderella marries the prince, her stepmother and stepsisters are punished, and Cinderella finds her happily ever after.

Now let's analyze the plot of the famous novel *To Kill a Mockingbird* by Harper Lee using Freytag's Pyramid:

1. **Exposition**: The story is set in the 1930s in a small southern town called Maycomb. The exposition introduces the main characters, including Scout Finch, her brother Jem, and their father Atticus Finch, a lawyer. It establishes the town's social dynamics and racial tensions.
2. **Rising Action**: The rising action includes Scout and Jem's growing curiosity about their reclusive neighbor, Boo Radley. It also involves the trial of Tom Robinson, a Black man falsely accused of raping a white woman, and Atticus's decision to defend him.
3. **Climax**: The climax occurs during Tom Robinson's trial. Atticus delivers a powerful closing argument, exposing the racial prejudice and injustice in the town. Despite the evidence in Tom's favor, the jury finds him guilty, reflecting the deeply ingrained racism of the time.
4. **Falling Action**: The falling action begins to resolve the story's conflicts and includes the aftermath of the trial, the children's encounters with Boo Radley, and the revelation of Boo's true nature as a protector.
5. **Resolution**: In *To Kill a Mockingbird*, the resolution involves Scout's realization about the importance of empathy and understanding, as well as her growing understanding of the complexities of the world around her. The story concludes with Boo Radley's reclusive nature and his subtle connection with Scout and Jem.

As a final example, let's analyze the plot of the film *The Shawshank Redemption* using Freytag's Pyramid:

1. **Exposition**: The story begins with the introduction of Andy Dufresne, a banker who is wrongfully convicted of murdering his wife and her lover. The exposition sets the stage by presenting Andy's arrival at Shawshank State Penitentiary, where he encounters the harsh prison environment and meets various inmates, including Red, who becomes his close friend.

2. **Rising Action**: The rising action includes Andy's struggle to adapt to prison life, his growing friendship with Red, and his use of his financial skills to gain favor with the prison staff and fellow inmates. Andy also embarks on a long-term plan to escape from Shawshank.

3. **Climax**: The climax occurs when Andy successfully escapes from Shawshank State Penitentiary. The moment of truth is revealed when the prison authorities discover Andy's escape and realize the extent of his meticulous plan.

4. **Falling Action**: The falling action includes the aftermath of Andy's escape, the revelation of corruption within the prison system, and the impact Andy's actions have on the lives of both the inmates and the prison staff.

5. **Resolution**: The resolution occurs when Red, who has been paroled, follows the instructions left by Andy and finds him in Zihuatanejo, Mexico. The story concludes with their reunion and the promise of a new life for both of them.

Here's a story I wrote about my life that employs Freytag's Pyramid:

Exposition:

My son Charlie was moving to New York from California to start his new life, a new job, a new home, everything. As his father, I struggled to process the fact that he wouldn't be living with us anymore. We decided to go on a road trip together, just he and I, to New York—a fun and interesting road trip that harkened back to the hundreds of other road trips we had taken when he was growing up, but this one was different. He wouldn't be coming back home with me after this one. The trip was bittersweet, filled with nostalgia and the weight of impending separation.

Rising Action:

As we journeyed across the country, I grappled with conflicting emotions of pride in Charlie's independence and the sadness of letting him go. I reminisced about our past road trips and the memories we shared, but the realization that this trip marked a permanent change in our lives loomed over me. The words "the best is yet to come" echoed in my mind, a mantra I had heard all my life from my mother and grandmother and a phrase from a popular Frank Sinatra song. It was a guiding force in our family, and it gave me hope during this emotional time. The road trip became a cathartic experience for both Charlie and me. We bonded over shared memories and created new ones, but the impending separation cast a shadow over our adventures. I struggled with the loss of my own mother, and I could see how much Charlie missed his Nana more than anything. The weight of her absence added an extra layer of emotional complexity to the journey.

Climax:

Upon arriving in New York, Charlie and I shared a final dinner in Chinatown, a place that held deep sentimental value for our family. As we sat together, the weight of the imminent farewell hung heavily in the air. When the bill came and we each cracked open our fortune cookies, I was stunned to read, "the best is yet to come." Those six words held a deep significance for me, reinforcing the mantra that had guided my family for generations and reminding me of Charlie's close bond with my mother.

Falling Action:

As we prepared to part ways at the airport the next day, I thought of those words and found solace in the idea that this departure marked the start of a new and exciting chapter for Charlie. I was comforted by the notion that our family's legacy of love, resilience, and hope would continue to guide us both. With a heavy heart and a hopeful spirit, I left the airport, carrying with me the belief that "the best is yet to come" and looking forward to the future with a renewed sense of optimism and purpose.

Resolution:

Looking back on that moment, I'm convinced that both my mother and grandmother were there for me and for Charlie as well. They were letting us know it was okay to say goodbye, that this next phase of life had arrived, and that we needed to embrace it. It's one of the most profound things I've ever experienced as a father. And even though I miss seeing him every day (but look forward to every call or visit), I think of those words, and I know that he will continue to thrive and that the best truly is yet to come.

Something else about Freytag's Pyramid: while this structure provides a tried-and-true framework for crafting a compelling narrative, it doesn't necessarily have to be followed in a rigid, linear manner. In fact, one of the beauties of storytelling is the ability to play with structure to create an unexpected and engaging flow. As a memoir writer, you have the creative license to rearrange these elements to suit your narrative needs. For instance, you might open with a dramatic scene that serves as a glimpse of the climax, then backtrack to the exposition before delving into the rising action. This nonlinear approach can add intrigue and mystery to your memoir, captivating your readers in a unique way.

By strategically rearranging the elements of Freytag's pyramid, you can subvert expectations, build tension, and keep your readers on their toes. Just remember, the key is to maintain coherence and ensure that the narrative remains compelling and easy to follow, even if the chronological order is disrupted. So, feel free to experiment with the structure, and let your memoir take on a captivating and unexpected form that keeps your readers eagerly turning the pages. After all, the beauty of storytelling lies in its endless possibilities!

Here are a couple of examples to illustrate a nonlinear approach:

Example 1: Starting with the Ending

Imagine opening your memoir with a poignant scene that depicts a significant moment from the conclusion of your story. Perhaps it's an emotional reunion with a long-lost family member, or a pivotal decision that shapes the course of your life. By beginning with this climactic moment, you immediately pique the reader's curiosity and create a sense of anticipation. From there, you can backtrack to the exposition and rising action to gradually reveal how you arrived at this impactful juncture in your life. This approach can effectively hook readers from the outset and keep them engaged as they eagerly seek to understand the events leading up to the powerful scene with which you started.

Example 2: Starting with the Climax

Alternatively, you might opt to kick off your memoir with the climax itself—a moment of intense conflict, revelation, or transformation that serves as a narrative focal point. By plunging readers directly into the heart of the action, you immediately grab their attention and immerse them in the emotional and dramatic core of your story. After setting the stage with this gripping opening, you can then skillfully weave in the exposition and rising action to provide context and depth, gradually leading up to the climactic moment that readers initially encountered. This approach can create a sense of immediacy and intensity, drawing readers into the heart of your memoir from the very first page.

By starting with the ending or the climax, you can captivate readers with the promise of a compelling journey, prompting them to delve deeper into your memoir to uncover the rich tapestry of experiences and emotions that lead to the powerful moments with which you chose to begin.

While Freytag's Pyramid is widely recognized and effective, it is not the only option available. Every writer has their own preferences and unique storytelling style. Exploring different formulas and approaches allows you to find the one that resonates with you the most and suits your story's needs.

Additionally, storytelling is an art form with endless possibilities. You are not limited to existing formulas, and there is no fixed rulebook that must be followed. Feel free to experiment, create your own hybrid structures, or even challenge traditional storytelling conventions. It's through this exploration and innovation that new and exciting narrative techniques emerge.

The key is to find a storytelling approach that serves your story and engages your audience. Whether you prefer a classic structure, an experimental narrative, or a fusion of different techniques, the ultimate goal is to captivate readers and deliver a compelling and memorable story.

So don't be afraid to think outside the box, adapt existing formulas to suit your needs, or even create your own storytelling style. The possibilities are truly limitless, and embracing your unique voice and vision can lead to extraordinary storytelling experiences. Remember, storytelling is an art, and it's in the exploration and expression of your creativity that the magic truly happens.

THE 500-WORD STORY CHALLENGE

One assignment I've given writers in my memoir workshop since day one has been the 500-word story. It's very basic. After you create a list of prominent and seminal moments in your life, choose one and craft a 500-word story based on that particular event or moment in your life. Use the five steps of

Freytag's Pyramid, "show, don't tell," and practice good descriptive writing.

My students will come back with, "Five hundred words is not enough space to do that." I disagree. I actually think it's a productive challenge because it forces you to fit a lot of good information within a fairly tight construct. Fitting a solid story in 500 words not only forces you to focus on efficiency and word economy, but it also helps you hone your editing skills (since you'll probably be whittling down a first draft to meet the 500-word goal).

The number 500 wasn't arbitrary for me. It's an exercise I came up with out of necessity. Typically, I would have between twenty and twenty-five students in a workshop and everybody was interested in getting up to read the week after the assignment was given. Practically speaking, there would never have been enough time to include everyone if the stories were not compact and succinct. What I realized after a couple of years was that the 500-word challenge was actually very helpful, because it gave writers the framework and blueprint of a bigger, unpacked story (should they care to tell it). It's like cooking for one person: if you can master the recipe for one, then you can do it for any amount. You just keep doubling the amount you need based on the number of people you're serving.

In other words, a 500-word story can easily become a 5,000-word story—if you take each level of the pyramid, expand it, and unpack it more. A 500-word story could even become a 50,000-word book if the story moves you.

Below is an example of a story I shared with one of my groups. I'm not saying it's a great or perfectly told story, but it's an episode of my life that I remembered in great detail. I recall a lot from this particular day; there are many little conflicts and resolutions that took place that I thought would be fun to include in a longer piece. I've also included a photo with the story, which I reference. It's important whenever possible to incorporate a visual aid to help bring things even more to life.

As far as a 500-word assignment goes, this gave me a good starting point to begin making sense of why this moment mattered so much to me. The exercise allowed me to explore all five portions of the pyramid—but more importantly, it gave me a solid outline, should I ever want to expand the story into something deeper.

I was about eleven years old when my dad arranged for us to visit the New York Giants football training camp in 1973, then held at a college in Monmouth, New Jersey. While my dad had lunch with the team owners and Howard Cosell, I was basically left to fend for myself out on the fresh-cut green grass field surrounded by behemoths in blue and white jerseys. The sounds of coaches' whistles near and far, pads crashing into metal tackling sleds, and players barking play options filled the air. In all of this activity, I was alone. Then, I heard a voice.

"Hey, little man, let's get you doing something..." I turned and saw number 43. Carl "Spider" Lockhart, grinning down at me. My favorite Giant, in the flesh. Arm draped around my shoulder, he took me around the field, he let me set up balls on the tee so the kicker Pete Gogolak could practice. He showed me how to run a couple of patterns, and he made me feel like I belonged.

Afterward, in the player cafeteria, Spider made sure I had a seat right next to him. The players ate like wolves, devouring the meats, chicken, vegetables, and entire loaves of bread like men condemned. Soon, Spider led me around the room to meet every single player so I could get autographs on my media guide. Because I was with Spider, every player stopped what they were doing, shook my hand, and asked me about myself.

I have a picture of us in the parking lot right before we said goodbye. I don't think I'd ever been happier in my life. A few weeks later, we were at Yankee Stadium to watch the Giants play. Lockhart (a safety) intercepted a pass and ran it back for a touchdown. I was thrilled. We got to go to the locker room after the game, and when he saw me, he rushed over. "Little man!" he said and asked me what I thought of his touchdown play. I told him it was amazing and then he explained to me exactly how he read the play, picked off the pass, and ran it back.

In July 1986, I was on a subway in New York City reading the paper... When I saw the *New York Post* obituary, that day came back to me, and I just started crying there on the train.... Spider, just forty-three years old, had died of cancer.

There was an innocence to that time that seems somewhat lost today. It's hard to even imagine an experience like this happening today because of the layers of security and handlers and interests that are drawn to a big-money sport. I'm so thankful that I wandered out alone on that field that hot late summer day. Had I not, I would never have been rescued by a decent, thoughtful man who sensed he could make a difference in a little boy's life that this now-grown man will never forget.

So now is the time. Go choose one of those ten moments that you outlined and write it as a story. Odds are you'll write a fairly effective, descriptive story that makes a reader feel like they're with you if you remember these key things:

Select a specific moment or scene: Choose a single moment or scene that encapsulates the essence of your story. This allows you to concentrate your descriptive efforts and create a picture within a limited word count.

Use sensory details: Engage the reader's senses by incorporating descriptive language that appeals to sight, sound, taste, touch, and smell. These details can bring the narrative to life and make it more immersive.

Show, don't tell: Instead of straightforwardly stating emotions or experiences, show them through actions, dialogue, and observations. This allows readers to draw their own conclusions and become more engaged in the story.

Focus on significant details: In a limited word count, prioritize the details that are most crucial to the narrative and its impact. Choose details that reveal character, advance the plot, or evoke a strong emotional response.

Create a strong narrative voice: The first-person perspective offers an opportunity to develop a distinctive narrative voice. Use this voice to convey emotions, thoughts, and insights.

Structure your story effectively: With a concise word count, structure becomes even more critical. Consider employing a clear beginning, middle, and end, and ensure that each paragraph or section contributes to the overall narrative arc.

Edit and revise ruthlessly: As with any form of writing, the editing process is crucial. Review your story and trim unnecessary words, refine descriptions, and strengthen the impact of each sentence. Every word must count in a 500-word narrative.

Remember that the goal is not to tell an expansive or comprehensive story, but to create a concise snapshot that leaves a lasting impression on the audience. By employing these strategies and making deliberate choices in your storytelling, you can indeed write an effective and descriptive first-person narrative within 500 words.

You know the basics about how to write a story. Now do it. From this point on, it only gets better.

A PAIR OF JOHN CHEEVER MEMORIES

John Cheever's study was a sanctuary of creativity. The room exuded an air of quiet contemplation and intellectual energy. I couldn't help but be in awe of the well-oiled machinery of his writing life. The walls were lined with bookshelves that were filled to the brim with volumes of literature I had only dreamed of reading. A typewriter sat prominently on his desk—a testament to the bygone era of writing before the rise of computers.

When we sat down together, Mr. Cheever would take out my stories, his red felt-tip marker poised to make notes in the margins. His feedback was invaluable, and I hung on to his every word. He would offer suggestions and insights that transformed my writing, urging me to dig deeper into my characters or to create more evocative descriptions. "Make her more mysterious," he would say, or "Describe the flowers in the garden, and as they are dying, let that serve as a metaphor for the relationship." His guidance breathed life into my stories, adding layers of complexity and nuance that I had never considered.

During these sessions, there were moments of silence. Mr. Cheever would light cigarette after cigarette, the smoke curling lazily in the air as he gazed out the window, lost in thought. I marveled at the weight of his contemplation, knowing that I was witnessing a glimpse into the mind of a true storytelling master.

Occasionally, our conversations would veer off into other topics, like baseball or current events. These casual exchanges provided a glimpse into the man behind the writer—a person with a wide range of interests and a genuine curiosity about the world. It was during these moments that I realized the importance of being well-rounded and knowledgeable in order to enrich one's writing.

I remember one afternoon clearly. The sun was casting a warm glow over Mr. Cheever's study. As we settled in for our regular meeting, Mr. Cheever wore a solemn expression. I sensed a heaviness in his voice. He began to recount a recent phone call—a notification that shattered his world for a brief moment. It was news of the tragic demise of his dear friend and fellow author, John Updike. The words hung heavy in the air, carrying the weight of sorrow and disbelief.

However, as the story unraveled, it became apparent that the news of Updike's passing was an unfortunate fabrication. A mistake. Evidently there was another John Updike who had passed. Despite this revelation, Cheever's emotions remained raw, his thoughts still consumed by the idea of loss and mortality.

For the duration of our meeting that day, Mr. Cheever spoke with eloquence and passion, his words flowing into the depths of his own reflections on life's transience, the fragility of the human condition, and the inevitability of our mortal existence.

Amidst the contemplation of mortality, one theme stood out prominently in Mr. Cheever's discourse—his admiration for John Updike's writing. He spoke of Updike's unparalleled talent, his ability to capture the nuances of life with his pen.

Near the end of our session, Mr. Cheever leaned forward slightly, his eyes locking with mine. With an earnestness I can still recall, he imparted his wisdom, the best advice he believed he could offer. "Read Updike," he said, his voice filled with conviction. "Forget about me. Just go read Updike. You will learn everything you need to know about great writing."

That night in our small library at home, I grabbed my father's copy of *Rabbit, Run* and began reading at once.

John Updike remains a favorite author of mine to this day.

Another time, on a late Sunday afternoon, I had made plans to visit Mr. Cheever. At the time, I was about sixteen years old and able to drive. He called me and inquired, "Do you ice skate?" I told him I did, recalling the occasional small makeshift hockey games my friends and I played on the nearby Teatown Lake, just down Spring Valley Road. "How about we ice skate then?" I picked him up, and we drove down to the lake.

Upon arrival, we found a small dock where we sat and laced up our skates. The vast lake lay empty, its surface pristine as it hadn't snowed for a while. The late winter afternoon was adorned with layers of purple clouds that obscured the setting orange sun. As we glided across the ice, I couldn't help but observe the great novelist John Cheever as he effortlessly maneuvered, even in his mid-sixties and seeming a bit older than that, he was quite graceful and controlled. His movements were like a dance on the ice, a testament to his grace and poise.

The only sounds were the rhythmic scraping of our blades, and we didn't talk much as we skated. After about an hour, we skated back to the dock and put our shoes back on. It was here that Cheever shared, "Skating is a good way for me to clear my head. That helps me write." As I reflected on his words, it became clear that this experience served as a lesson—a reminder to find outlets like skating that help open the mind and foster creativity, especially in the pursuit of writing. I realized that moments like these, where the mind is free and the body is in motion, can be invaluable for nurturing the creative spirit.

CHAPTER 8

Reading, Vocabulary, and Recording Yourself

Often in a memoir workshop, I start by asking students a vital question: What books are you currently reading? If the answer is "none," I must admit, I take issue. You see, reading and writing go hand in hand. They're an inseparable duo. So, allow me to emphasize why reading is so essential for honing your writing skills.

First and foremost, reading expands our vocabulary. Every book we read introduces us to a plethora of words and phrases. By exploring different writing styles and genres, we can enrich our lexicon and discover new ways to express our thoughts and ideas. A robust vocabulary enables us to communicate with greater precision and nuance, elevating the quality of our writing.

Through reading, we absorb correct grammar usage and proper sentence structure almost effortlessly. As we immerse ourselves in various texts, we develop an intuitive understanding of how language works. This knowledge enables us to construct more coherent and polished sentences in our own writing, ensuring that our ideas are conveyed effectively.

But reading is not merely a passive exercise—it's an opportunity to observe and learn from skilled writers. As we explore diverse authors and genres, we encounter different writing styles and techniques. We witness how successful writers craft engaging narratives, develop compelling characters, and employ literary devices. By attentively analyzing and studying these techniques, we can integrate them into our own writing, making our words more captivating and powerful.

Reading also sparks our imagination and nurtures our creativity. When we immerse ourselves in books, we are transported to imaginative worlds, exposed to unique perspectives, and introduced to new ideas. This exposure encourages us to think beyond the ordinary and explore innovative approaches to storytelling. By incorporating this sense of imagination into our writing, we can create works that are more original, vibrant, and thought-provoking.

Let's not forget that reading also expands our knowledge. Through books, we gain access to a vast array of subjects and topics. We deepen our understanding of the world, encounter new concepts, and broaden our horizons. This expanded knowledge base empowers us to write with authority, credibility, and depth on various subjects, enriching the quality of our work.

Essential storytelling skills are acquired through reading. By exploring different narratives, we can dissect the structures, analyze plot developments, and study character arcs. When we read, we learn how to build suspense, create relatable characters, and craft interesting storylines. These storytelling elements become the building blocks of our own narratives, enabling us to construct stronger plots and develop more compelling characters.

Reading also nurtures our critical thinking and analytical skills. When we read, we actively engage with the text, analyze its content, and evaluate the effectiveness of the writing. This type of critical thinking becomes ingrained in our approach to writing, allowing us to refine our ideas, enhance clarity, and ensure coherence in our work.

Lastly, and perhaps most importantly, reading is a wellspring of inspiration and motivation. Engaging with well-crafted literature can ignite our passion for writing, provide us with new ideas, and remind us of the major impact that words can have. It fuels our drive to strive for excellence, pushing us as writers to constantly improve our craft.

VOCABULARY MATTERS

When teaching a memoir workshop, I stress the importance of continuously improving your vocabulary. A rich vocabulary allows you to express yourself more precisely and creatively, enhancing the quality of your writing. Fortunately, in today's technologically advanced world, there are numerous easy and accessible ways to expand your vocabulary through apps, games, and other resources.

A broader vocabulary provides you with a wider range of words and phrases to choose from, enabling you to convey your thoughts and emotions more effectively. Improving your vocabulary allows you to paint strong pictures with words, adding depth and nuance to your writing. By finding the precise words that capture your experiences, you can make your memoir more memorable for readers.

Effective communication is essential when sharing personal stories and experiences. Building your vocabulary helps you articulate your ideas with clarity and precision, allowing you to avoid ambiguity and ensuring that readers understand your intended meaning. As a result, your memoir becomes more accessible and relatable to a broader audience.

With an expanded vocabulary, you can choose words that create powerful imagery and sensory experiences. Descriptive language helps readers visualize the people, places, and events in your memoir, making it more immersive.

A diverse vocabulary enables you to experiment with different tones and writing styles. By accessing a broader range of words, you can adapt your writing to suit the tone and mood you want to convey in specific scenes or chapters. This versatility adds depth and complexity to your memoir, making it more dynamic and enjoyable to read.

Now, let's explore some easy ways to improve your vocabulary:

Vocabulary Apps: There are numerous vocabulary-building apps available for smartphones and tablets. These apps provide word quizzes, flashcards, and interactive exercises to help you learn new words and reinforce your understanding. Wordela, Promova, and Memrise, as of this writing, are three apps I consider to be quite good.

Reading: Reading widely exposes you to different styles of writing and introduces you to new words in context. Choose books, newspapers, and magazines that interest you and challenge your vocabulary. When you encounter unfamiliar words, make a habit of looking them up and understanding their meanings. You can also keep a vocabulary journal to note down new words and review them regularly.

Word Games and Puzzles: Engaging in word games and puzzles can be both fun and educational. Crossword puzzles, word searches, and Scrabble are excellent options for expanding your vocabulary while enjoying yourself. Many online platforms and mobile apps offer word games that cater to various skill levels. Me? I start each day playing Wordle, I also enjoy Wordscapes and Quordle among several others.

Vocabulary-Building Websites: Numerous websites provide word-of-the-day features, vocabulary quizzes, and interactive exercises. Websites like Vocabulary.com, Merriam-Webster, and Dictionary.com offer valuable resources to help you improve your vocabulary.

Remember, improving your vocabulary is an ongoing process. Consistency and regular exposure to unfamiliar words are key. By incorporating these easy methods into your daily routine, you can steadily enhance your vocabulary and elevate your memoir-writing skills. I still try and learn at least one new word every day.

RECORD YOURSELF

I want to recommend another helpful technique for improving your writing skills. It's as simple as this: record yourself as you finish certain stories, then listen back to how you told those stories. With the convenience of smartphones and other related devices, it's incredibly easy to record yourself and take advantage of this powerful learning tool. By listening to your own story-telling, you can gain valuable insights into your writing. When reading silently, we may overlook certain aspects of our work. However, hearing our stories aloud brings a fresh perspective. This exercise allows you to identify areas where your writing could be more descriptive and captivating.

As you listen to the recordings, pay close attention to the flow and pacing of your story, as well as the overall impact of your words. Take note of sections that feel flat or lack detail. This exercise can help you recognize where you might need to add more sensory descriptions or incorporate stronger verbs to bring your scenes to life.

Recording yourself also helps catch any inconsistencies or gaps in your storytelling. By listening carefully, you can identify moments where the narrative seems disjointed or where additional context is needed. This enables you to refine the structure of your memoir and ensure that each story flows seamlessly.

Hearing your own voice narrating the stories allows you to gauge the emotional impact of your writing. You can sense whether the intended emotions are effectively conveyed, or if certain passages lack the desired impact. This exercise empowers you to revise and polish your memoir to elicit the desired response from your readers.

Remember, recording yourself and listening to your story-telling is an invaluable tool for anyone working on their memoir. It provides you with a valuable self-critique, helping you step back and objectively evaluate your work. Using this method also allows you to identify areas for improvement, refine your writing style, and ultimately create a more captivating and compelling memoir.

WORKING WITH DAVE MASON

Cowriting Dave Mason's memoir was an exhilarating yet challenging experience. As a legendary rock 'n' roll singer, songwriter, and guitar player, Dave was initially reticent to dive too deeply into his personal life. His guarded nature meant that unlocking his story required creating a trusting environment where he felt comfortable enough to share.

One of the significant challenges I faced was gaining Dave's trust and encouraging him to open up. It took time and patience to build a rapport with him and establish a relationship based on mutual respect and understanding. I had to assure him that his story would be treated with care and respect, and that his voice would be preserved throughout the memoir.

Another obstacle was Dave's memory. Over time, certain details had become hazy or forgotten. To overcome this, I conducted extensive research and dug deep into his past. By providing him with memory cues and triggers, I was able to transport him back to specific time periods and reignite his recollections. It was a fascinating process to witness as Dave's memories resurfaced, and he began to recall precise details and stories from his life.

Through this process, I learned that research and reaching out to people who were present during significant moments in one's life can be invaluable. These individuals can provide unique perspectives and trigger memories that may have been buried deep within. This approach can be helpful for anyone seeking to recall their own personal stories, as it allows for a more comprehensive and accurate recollection of events.

Cowriting Dave Mason's memoir was a rewarding experience. It demanded patience, trust-building, and thorough research. By creating a safe space for Dave to share his story and utilizing memory cues, I was able to help him unlock and preserve his remarkable career as a musician.

CHAPTER 9

In-Person Storytelling

Improving your in-person storytelling skills can greatly enhance your writing process. The ability to tell a story effectively allows you to communicate your thoughts, experiences, and emotions in a more engaging and compelling manner. This skill can help you articulate your ideas more clearly in your memoir and make your writing more captivating for readers.

When you tell a story in person, you have the opportunity to observe the reactions and engagement of your listeners. This direct interaction can provide valuable feedback on which elements of your story connect with people and which parts may need improvement. Understanding what captivates an audience can help you refine your storytelling techniques in your written memoir.

Storytelling in person often requires organizing your thoughts and experiences into a coherent narrative that has a clear beginning, middle, and end. This practice can help you develop a sense of structure and flow, which are essential elements in memoir writing. By honing your storytelling skills, you'll naturally become more adept at crafting a well-structured memoir.

Stories that evoke emotions have a profound impact on listeners. When you tell a story in person, you can gauge the emotional responses of your audience and adjust your storytelling techniques accordingly. Having awareness of emotional impact can translate into your writing, allowing you to create a more emotionally resonant narrative.

Storytelling in person often relies on your personal experiences, voice, and unique perspective. By practicing storytelling, you can develop your authentic voice and refine your ability to convey your own experiences and emotions. This individuality will shine through in your memoir, making it more relatable to readers.

Becoming a better storyteller in person can sharpen your written skills, improve your communication abilities, and refine your writing techniques. So, don't hesitate to practice and share your stories with others as you work on your memoir.

HOW TO TELL A BETTER STORY

Here are some tips for being a good storyteller:

Know your audience: Before you start telling a story, take some time to consider who your audience is and what their interests and preferences might be. This can help you tailor your storytelling approach to better engage your listeners.

Be authentic: Authenticity is key to being a good storyteller. Be true to your own voice and style, and avoid trying to imitate someone else's storytelling style or voice.

Use descriptive language: Good storytellers use descriptive language to create strong images in the listener's mind. Use sensory details like sights, sounds, smells, and textures to bring your story to life.

Build suspense: One of the most effective ways to keep your audience engaged is to build suspense throughout your story. Use cliffhangers, unexpected twists, and moments of tension to keep your listeners on the edge of their seats.

Practice pacing: Pacing is an important aspect of storytelling. It's important to find a rhythm that works for you and your audience, occasionally varying the pace of your storytelling to keep things interesting.

Emphasize emotion: Good stories evoke emotion in the listener—whether it's laughter, tears, or excitement. Use your own emotions to convey the feelings and emotions of your characters or subjects.

Be concise: While it's important to be descriptive, it's also important to be concise. Avoid rambling or going off on tangents, and focus on telling a tight, well-structured story.

Practice, practice, practice: Like any skill, storytelling takes practice. Take every opportunity to tell stories, whether it's at family gatherings, social events, or other public settings. The more you practice, the better you'll become.

Being a good storyteller involves a combination of preparation, practice, and a willingness to connect with your audience on a deep emotional level. By focusing on these key elements, you can become a masterful storyteller that captivates and inspires your listeners.

The qualities of a great storyteller can vary depending on the medium and context of the storytelling; however, there are some key qualities that are generally associated with effective storytelling:

Imagination: A great storyteller is able to use their imagination to create compelling stories that transport their audience to another time and place. They are able to create characters, settings, and scenarios that are believable, captivating, and draw their audience into the story.

Clarity: A great storyteller is able to communicate their message clearly and effectively, using language and imagery that is easy to understand and listen to. They convey complex ideas and emotions in a way that is accessible and relatable.

Empathy: A great storyteller is able to connect with their audience on an emotional level by showing empathy and understanding for their audience's experiences and perspectives. They create a sense of trust and rapport with their audience, which allows them to engage more deeply with their story.

Timing and pacing: A great storyteller is able to use timing and pacing to build suspense, create tension, and maintain the interest of their audience. They know when to speed up the pace of the story or slow down—and when to pause for effect—to keep their audience engaged and invested in the story.

A great storyteller is someone who is able to engage and captivate their audience through their imagination, clarity, empathy, and skillful use of timing and pacing. When you build that into your writing, your memoir will become even more powerful and memorable.

Here's a story of mine I've never shared before. It's personal, but it's a moment that illustrates an important event in my life that allows me to lean on basic storytelling techniques.

My heart was racing uncontrollably, each beat feeling like a thunderous drum reverberating through my chest, a relentless rhythm that refused to slow. There was an undeniable sense of wrongness, an ominous feeling that gnawed at the edges of my mind, urging me to seek help. So, we hurried to the emergency room, the stark, antiseptic scent of the hospital assaulting my senses as we entered.

Concerned doctors and nurses swarmed around me, their voices a cacophony of urgency and reassurance. Their grave expressions spoke volumes, and it was then that I learned the magnitude of my condition. "You're in the middle of a serious a-fib episode," they explained, their words landing heavily in the air. After several consultations and hushed conversations, they delivered the verdict: I needed a procedure to reset my heart's rhythm, a precarious endeavor that filled me with a bone-deep terror.

My kids were there, their anxious faces etched with worry, and my mother stood by, her eyes reflecting a mix of fear and unwavering love. My wife, my rock, held my hand tightly, her silent strength grounding me even as my mind threatened to spiral into the abyss of darkness. In that moment, surrounded by the ones I cherished most, I couldn't shake the haunting thought that this could be the end.

I signed the necessary papers, my trembling hand scrawling my consent, a weighty acknowledgment of the perilous path ahead. As the medical team prepared for the procedure, I was overcome by a sense of profound vulnerability, the sterile hospital room closing in around me like a suffocating shroud.

As the anesthesiologist prepared to administer the medication, a sense of weightlessness washed over me, accompanied by a disorienting lightheadedness that blurred the edges of my consciousness. The cold space faded into a hazy tableau, and before I knew it, I found myself adrift in a surreal dreamscape, suspended weightlessly high above the earth.

The view before me was nothing short of breathtaking—an astronaut's vantage point, with the radiant curve of the earth stretching out beneath me, a mosaic of vibrant blues and whites against the backdrop of the boundless expanse of outer space. It was a vision of unparalleled beauty, one that inspired a sense of awe and wonder beyond the confines of reality.

As I marveled at the iridescent jewel of our planet, a calm settled over me, the ethereal quiet broken only by the distant whispers of celestial bodies dancing in the cosmic ballet. In that suspended moment, I felt an inexplicable connection to the universe, a profound awareness of my place in the grand tapestry of existence.

Amidst the surreal serenity, a figure materialized behind me, and as I turned, I beheld the unmistakable countenance of Jerry Garcia, his presence suffused with a gentle warmth that transcended mortal understanding. "I know you're scared," he murmured, his voice a soothing balm to my frayed nerves. "But you're not alone. We're here to help."

As he spoke, the space around us shimmered and shifted, and before long, the rest of the Grateful Dead band appeared, their presence suffusing the environment with an otherworldly warmth.

"Call the tune," Jerry encouraged, his voice resonating with a quiet strength. "We'll get you through this."

"Ripple," I whispered, the word escaping my lips like a fervent prayer. And as the familiar strains of the song filled the cosmos, a peacefulness enveloped me, infusing my being with a radiant tranquility that transcended the boundaries of the physical world.

As the song wrapped me in its tender embrace, I felt a connection to something greater than myself, a force that bound us all together in a tapestry of shared humanity. And as the final notes faded into the infinite distance, I surrendered to the healing embrace, allowing its ineffable strength to carry me through the tumultuous currents of my darkest fears. In that moment, I also realized the significance of the song's title - like a ripple spreading across a tranquil pond, it symbolized the outward flow of energy and the subtle but persistent movement forward. Although I hadn't consciously chosen the song for its metaphorical meaning, its message of progress and renewal resonated deeply with me.

As I emerged from the depths of unconsciousness, the steady beeping of medical equipment filled the air, and the concerned faces of my family members swam into focus. In that moment, I knew that I had crossed a threshold, emerging from the crucible of fear.

Throughout the arduous journey of recovery, I carried with me the echoes of that encounter, a testament to the unyielding strength that resides within the human spirit and the transcendent ability of music to uplift, heal, and guide us through the darkest of times. And as I took my first tentative steps toward recovery, I knew that I would forever be buoyed by the rock-solid support of my loved ones and the timeless melodies that had carried me through the abyss and into the light.

In the days that followed, as I gradually regained my vitality, the memory of that transcendent encounter remained etched in my mind, a beacon of hope that illuminated even the most foreboding moments. The love and support of my family enveloped me like a warm embrace, and the healing power of music became an integral part of my journey toward recovery.

As I stood on the threshold of a new beginning, I carried the understanding that even in the face of adversity, hope and healing could blossom like fragile petals reaching for the sun. The encounter, where the lines of reality blurred and the timeless strains of music guided me through the depths of fear, became a testament to the indomitable strength of the enduring resonance of love and connection.

THE SHORT STORIES OF JOHN CHEEVER

John Cheever's collection of short stories, *The Stories of John Cheever*, has always held a special place in my heart. It became a favorite book of mine after its release in 1978, and remains so to this day. I first discovered these stories while he was still alive, but it was during my college years in the early 1980s—shortly after his passing—that I truly became attached to this remarkable collection.

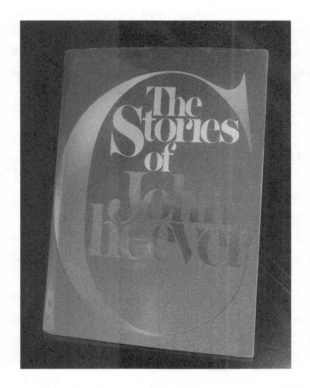

I remember one day at his house. As I entered his study, my eyes were immediately drawn to a box sitting prominently on his desk. It was filled with copies of this then-new collection, their iconic red covers gleaming under the soft glow of the room's ambient lighting. "You might enjoy some of these," he said, reaching into the box and handing me one of his soon-to-be bestsellers. The collection would win the Pulitzer Prize the following year.

What makes Cheever's short stories so special? Well, for starters, his ability to capture the essence of human existence within the confines of a few pages is simply astounding. His characters come alive—their struggles, desires, and flaws laid bare for us to witness. Whether it's the yearning of a suburban housewife, the identity crisis of a man wrestling with societal expectations, or the disintegration of family bonds, Cheever's stories plunge deep into the universal themes that touch us all.

What truly sets Cheever apart is his keen eye for observation. His attention to detail and his ability to convey the nuances of everyday life are unparalleled. Through his precise and evocative prose, he paints powerful pictures of the worlds he creates—whether it's the meticulously manicured lawns of suburbia or the bustling streets of New York City. It is within these settings that his stories unfold, drawing us in and making us feel as though we are part of the narrative.

But it's not just his skill in capturing reality that makes his collection so beloved. Cheever effortlessly blends realism with elements of the surreal or unexpected. He seamlessly weaves together the ordinary and the extraordinary, infusing his stories with a sense of wonder and surprise. This unique blend keeps people on their toes, engaged and eager to uncover the hidden depths within.

Cheever's exploration of themes—such as identity, conformity, and the search for meaning—can strike a chord with folks from all walks of life. His stories get into the complexities of human relationships and the impact of societal expectations, offering insights into our own lives and experiences. Through the struggles and triumphs of his characters, he reveals universal truths.

But let's not forget the sheer beauty of Cheever's prose. His writing is elegant and exquisitely crafted. Each sentence is a work of art, blending simplicity with lyrical beauty. The rhythm and cadence of his words draw us in, allowing us to savor each line and immerse ourselves fully in the world he has created.

John Cheever's collection of short stories is a testament to his deep understanding of the human condition, his impeccable craftsmanship, and his ability to create stories that connect to readers on a deeply personal level. Within the pages of *The Stories of John Cheever*, I find solace, inspiration, and a reminder of the power of storytelling to illuminate the world around us.

WORKING WITH BRIAN WHEAT

Working with the bass player and original member of the popular band Tesla, presented me with a unique opportunity as a cowriter. Rock star memoirs are often rife with tales of excess and extreme bravado, but Brian is different. While he certainly indulged in the rock and roll lifestyle, he also grappled with a multitude of ailments, both physical and mental in nature. Depression, body image, and many other "non-rock star" topics provided a unique opportunity to present the story of a very unconventional rock star.

To Brian's credit, it was important for him to unpack these parts of his life, not only to help himself deal with them, but also as a message to others who are suffering in similar circumstances. He wanted them to know they were not alone, and that's always an important mantra in first-person narrative writing—reminding the reader that they are not alone.

As we delved into his story, I was struck by the depth of Brian's experiences. He was open and honest about the challenges he faced, both in the spotlight and behind the scenes. Through our collaboration, we were able to weave a narrative that showcased the complexities of his journey, offering a candid look at the highs and lows of life as a musician, but also delving into the deeply personal struggles that often go unspoken.

Brian's willingness to share his vulnerabilities was both courageous and inspiring. It became clear that his story was not just about the glamour of the music industry, but about the resilience and strength it takes to confront one's inner demons. His candid reflections on mental health, body image, and the pressures of fame added a profound layer of depth to our writing, resonating with readers on a deeply human level.

Through our collaboration, Brian's memoir became a testament to the power of honesty and vulnerability. It was a story that transcended the traditional rock and roll narrative, offering a message of hope and solidarity to anyone who has grappled with similar challenges. It was a privilege to work with Brian in bringing his story to life, and I am grateful for the opportunity to shine a light on the unspoken struggles of a truly unconventional rockstar.

CHAPTER 10

Unveiling the Tapestry
of Your Life

In the first nine chapters, you have learned the fundamental elements of crafting and telling a story. You may be surprised to discover that you already possess some essential building blocks needed to create a captivating memoir. But we have more to do.

Now the real work begins—the beautiful adventure of transformation through writing. From this point on, if you dedicate yourself to the practice of daily writing, you will refine your storytelling craft in ways you may never have felt plausible.

As you write, you will find yourself honing your skills and gradually perfecting the art of organizing and refining your narrative. It may seem overwhelming, but trust in the process. With each word, each sentence, and each chapter, you are advancing toward a memoir that exceeds even your wildest expectations.

Remember, this is just the beginning. There is still much to be done, but fret not; you are equipped with the knowledge to accomplish far more than you may presently imagine. Your story has potential and is waiting to be unveiled and shared with the world.

Now, we will dig deeper into the intricacies of crafting your memoir. We will explore the importance of tone and voice, the art of character development, and the transformative power of vulnerability—not to mention the development of scenes, characters, and narrative arcs.

The art of scene development is so important. Scenes are the building blocks of your memoir; they're the moments that take your readers into the heart of your story. In this chapter, we will learn how to craft vivid scenes that engage the senses, evoke emotions, and immerse your audience in the world you have experienced.

As for character development, your memoir is not solely about you; it is also about the people who have influenced and shaped your life. I will get into the techniques of bringing these characters to life on the page—describing their personalities, motivations, and impact on your story. Through their interactions, conflicts, and growth, we will create a multi-dimensional cast.

A memoir is not just a collection of moments; it is a cohesive narrative that takes the reader on a transformative trip. We will learn how to shape your memoir's narrative arc, ensuring that it has a compelling beginning, a well-paced middle, and a satisfying resolution. By understanding the power of structure and pacing, we will captivate readers and keep them eagerly turning the page.

THE FOCUS

Remember a memoir is not meant to encapsulate your entire life's story, but rather, to tackle a specific moment, time period, or theme that holds significance for you. By narrowing your focus, you harness the power of storytelling to convey a deeper truth and leave a lasting impression on your readers. By honing in on a particular experience or time period, you have the opportunity to explore the richness and complexity of that specific chapter in your life. It is within these boundaries that the true essence of your story can emerge, allowing you to paint a compelling picture.

As you select the focus of your memoir, consider the moments that hold the greatest potential for strong storytelling. Look for experiences that are ripe with emotions, conflicts, and personal growth. These are the moments that will captivate and draw people into your narrative, enabling them to connect with your story on a profound level.

As you craft your memoir, strive to uncover universal truths within your personal experiences. Your story has the power to reach folks far beyond the confinements of your own life. By exploring the themes and insights that emerge from your chosen focus, you can offer readers a deeper understanding of the human condition and create a sense of shared empathy and connection.

Again, your memoir is not just about recounting events; it is an opportunity to communicate the essence of your experiences and the wisdom you have gained along the way. By selecting a focused lens through which to tell your story, you can distill the essence of your narrative and leave your readers with a universal truth that transcends time and place.

As far as focus, here are some common areas that memoirs explore:

Childhood and Coming-of-Age: Many memoirs dive into the author's formative years, exploring their upbringing, family dynamics, and the experiences that shaped them into the person they are today. These memoirs often explore themes of identity, self-discovery, and the challenges of growing up.

Personal Journeys: Memoirs can also center around a personal journey or transformation. This might involve overcoming a personal struggle, such as addiction, illness, or trauma. These stories often focus on the author's path to healing, self-reflection, and personal growth.

Career and Professional Life: Some memoirs revolve around the author's career or professional accomplishments. These memoirs might provide insights into a particular industry, offer advice or lessons learned, or share behind-the-scenes stories from their professional life. They can be especially helpful for readers interested in a specific field or seeking guidance in their own careers.

Travel and Exploration: Memoirs about travel and exploration often take readers on trips to different parts of the world. These memoirs capture the author's experiences and encounters with different cultures, as well as the lessons they learned while on their adventures.

Relationships and Love: Memoirs that focus on relationships—whether romantic, familial, or friendships—explore the complexities and dynamics of human connections. These memoirs may broach topics such as love, loss, forgiveness, and personal connections. They often provide insight into the author's emotional experiences and the lessons they learned from their relationships.

Historical and Social Commentary: Some memoirs zero in on a specific historical period or societal issue. These memoirs can shed light on significant events, such as wars or political movements, and offer a personal perspective on the impact of these events on individuals and society. They often combine personal experiences with broader social and historical analysis.

Young Adulthood: Memoirs that concentrate on the transition from youth to adulthood often cover the author's experiences during their twenties and thirties. These memoirs may explore topics like career choices, establishing independence, navigating relationships, personal growth, and the challenges of early adulthood.

Adolescence and Teenage Years: Memoirs centered around adolescence and teenage years often explore the challenges, discoveries, and rites of passage that individuals experience during this formative period. They may include themes such as identity formation, peer pressure, sexuality, and the search for independence.

Midlife Reflections: Memoirs focusing on midlife can concentrate on the experiences, transitions, and self-reflection that occur during this stage. They may cover topics such as career changes, family dynamics, identity shifts, regrets, and reevaluating one's priorities and goals.

Retirement and Later Years: Memoirs centered around retirement and the later years of life can offer reflections on a lifetime of experiences, accomplishments, and lessons learned. They may cover topics like legacy, wisdom gained, aging, and finding purpose and fulfillment in the later stages of life.

Specific Life Events: Memoirs can also center on specific life events that have had a significant impact on the author. These events can range from personal milestones such as getting married, having children, or losing a loved one to extraordinary experiences like surviving a natural disaster, embarking on a long-distance hike, or participating in a life-altering adventure.

Spiritual or Philosophical Journeys: Some memoirs focus on the author's spiritual or philosophical sojourns. These memoirs explore their path to faith, belief systems, personal philosophies, or their search for meaning and purpose in life.

Remember, these are just a few examples. There are countless other periods of life that memoirists might choose to focus on. Because memoir writing allows authors to share their unique perspectives and experiences, the possibilities for subject matter are vast.

THIS IS THE TIME TO START ORGANIZING

Once you've identified which portion of your life your memoir will encompass, it's time to create a specific list of the stories within that timeframe. Don't hold back. Even if something initially seems insignificant, include it in your list anyway. You can always remove it later, if needed.

During this initial stage, throw everything into the pot from that particular time in your life. Now, one by one, begin writing each of those stories. The order in which you tackle them is entirely up to you, and can be influenced by your mood or whatever hits you at that moment. Thankfully, your stories don't have to be written in chronological order. Feel free to jump around and write the stories as they come to you.

Once you've finished writing those stories, the process of organizing them into a memoir begins. Here's the exciting part: the organization doesn't have to be chronological. You have the creative freedom to arrange the stories in a way that best serves your narrative and themes. Consider the emotional impact, thematic connections, or even a nonlinear structure that captures the essence of your experiences.

Think of your memoir as a puzzle. Organizing the stories is like finding the perfect arrangement of the pieces. You can experiment with different sequences, try various chapter structures, or even weave in recurring themes throughout the book. The goal is to create a cohesive and compelling narrative that captures the essence of your life.

Just remember that there's no one-size-fits-all approach. Give yourself the freedom to explore and experiment. Write the stories as they come to you, organize them in a way that feels right, and trust your creative instincts. Your memoir is a unique reflection of your life, and it's up to you to shape it into a compelling and meaningful narrative.

REMEMBER, THE PROCESS MATTERS MORE THAN MONEY

The process of writing your story allows you to mine the depths of your being, examining the joys, sorrows, triumphs, and challenges that have molded you. It's an opportunity to confront your fears and embrace the strength that lies within you. This journey of self-exploration and growth is invaluable, regardless of whether your story reaches a wide audience or remains tucked away in the pages of your journal.

Writing your story can be a cathartic release—a way to heal wounds, find closure, and express your truth. It's a means of reclaiming your voice, empowering yourself, and giving shape to the narratives that have defined your existence. The act of writing itself becomes a therapeutic process, offering solace, clarity, and a newfound sense of purpose.

While the desire to share your story with others is natural and understandable, it's essential to remember that the worth of your story does not lie solely in external validation or recognition. It's the internal transformation—the growth and fulfillment you experience along the way—that truly matters.

Writing your story may lead to unexpected outcomes. It may open doors to new opportunities, connections, or even publication. But even if those doors don't swing wide open, never underestimate the impact that your story can have on your own life and those closest to you. Your story has the power to inspire, empathize, and connect with others on a deeply human level.

So embrace the experience of writing your story wholeheartedly. Embrace the ups and downs, the moments of inspiration, and the challenges that may arise. Treasure the process of self-discovery and the growth that comes with it. True value lies not in external rewards but in the impact the process has on your own life. Your story matters, and the path you choose will be a transformative and empowering one.

WORKING WITH PHIL COLLEN

Working with Phil Collen from Def Leppard was a fascinating challenge. Collaborating with someone primarily known as the lead guitarist in a world-famous band presented a unique opportunity to explore the lesser-known facets of his life. Phil's desire to focus on aspects of his life away from the band was important to him, and it became equally important to me as his cowriter.

The lesson I learned from working with Phil was invaluable: don't always feel constrained to write about the obvious parts of your life. There are often lesser-known, yet equally compelling, stories that are important to share with the world. Phil's willingness to dig deep into those more personal anecdotes from his life served as a powerful reminder to encourage others to do the same.

Through our collaboration, I discovered the richness of Phil's experiences beyond his role in Def Leppard. His willingness to share those personal and often overlooked stories made for a memoir that was authentic, diverse, and deeply engaging. Working with Phil reminded me of the importance of embracing all aspects of one's life when crafting a memoir and not hesitating to dig deep into the less obvious facets that make each person's story unique.

CHAPTER 11

Outlining and Theme

When writing a memoir or a first-person narrative, creating an outline is like charting a course for your storytelling adventure. It serves as a valuable tool to guide you through the vast terrain of your memories and experiences. Let me explain why it's so vital.

First and foremost, an outline provides structure to your narrative. It acts as a road map, helping you organize your thoughts and arrange the events of your life in a logical and coherent manner. By outlining the key moments, themes, and emotions you want to explore, you create a framework that keeps your storytelling focused and on track.

Think of your outline as the backbone of your memoir. It gives your narrative strength and stability, ensuring that it flows smoothly from one chapter to the next. With a well-structured outline, you can avoid the pitfalls of meandering or losing your way while writing. The outline becomes a reliable guide, preventing you from getting overwhelmed by the vastness of your story.

An outline also helps maintain clarity and purpose throughout your writing process. By organizing your thoughts and memories, you can distill the essence of your experiences and convey them effectively. It enables you to stay true to the core message or theme of your narrative, ensuring that your readers connect with your story on a deeper level.

Creating an outline also allows you to identify gaps or missing pieces in your memoir. As you lay out the major events and milestones, you may discover areas that require further development or additional details. This awareness empowers you to fill in those gaps, resulting in a more comprehensive narrative.

An outline assists in pacing your story. It helps you determine the rhythm and tempo of your memoir, ensuring that it ebbs and flows in a way that readers will find captivating. By strategically placing moments of tension, reflection, and resolution along the timeline of your outline, you can create a dynamic and compelling narrative that keeps readers eagerly turning the pages.

Finally, an outline provides a sense of direction and purpose. It acts as a beacon that keeps you focused on your writing goals. When faced with writer's block or moments of uncertainty, your outline serves as a reference point, reminding you of the next step in your story. It offers a sense of confidence and reassurance, knowing that you have a clear path to follow.

Here are some tips to help you create an outline that serves as a strong foundation for your memoir:

Start with a brainstorming session: If you haven't already, start jotting down all the significant events, memories, and themes you want to include in your narrative. Don't worry about the order or structure at this stage—just focus on capturing all the essential elements.

Identify the main arc: Consider the overarching storyline or message you want to convey through your memoir. For instance, this could be a personal transformation or a series of life lessons. Determine the beginning, middle, and end of your narrative arc to create a sense of progression and development.

Organize chronologically or thematically: Decide whether you want to follow a chronological order, starting from your earliest memories and progressing through time, or if you prefer to organize your narrative thematically, grouping related events and experiences together. Choose the approach that best serves you and your story.

Break it down into chapters or sections: Divide your narrative into manageable sections or chapters. This helps create a sense of structure and allows for a more focused examination of each aspect of your story. Consider the natural breaks or transitions within your narrative that lend themselves to chapter divisions.

Be flexible: Remember that your outline is a flexible tool that can be adjusted as you dig deeper into your memoir. It's okay to modify the order of events or add/remove sections based on how your story unfolds. Stay open to new insights and ideas that may arise during the writing process.

Include key moments and emotional arcs: Within each section or chapter, highlight the key events and emotional arcs that drive your narrative forward. These moments could be pivotal turning points, challenges, triumphs, or moments of self-reflection. Ensure that each chapter has a purpose and contributes to the overall story.

Use descriptive headings: Craft clear and descriptive headings for each section or chapter of your outline. These headings should give you a sense of what each section covers at a glance. They will also serve as helpful signposts when you refer back to your outline during the writing process.

Leave room for exploration: While an outline provides structure, allow yourself the freedom to explore and discover new insights as you write. Your outline is a guide, but it's not set in stone. Embrace the creative process and be open to making adjustments as needed.

Remember, an outline is a tool to assist you in organizing your thoughts and ensuring a cohesive narrative. It's there to support you, but don't feel constrained by it. Adapt and refine your outline as you progress, and let your story unfold naturally.

TYPES OF OUTLINES

There are a variety of outlines to choose from. Keep in mind that these outlines are adaptable, and can be modified according to your specific needs and preferences.

Chronological Outline: This is the most straightforward and traditional approach to outlining a memoir. It follows a chronological order, starting from the beginning of your life or a specific time period, and moves through time until the end of the story. This outline helps to capture the arc of your life, allowing readers to witness the progression of events and experiences.

Thematic Outline: Instead of following a strict chronological structure, a thematic outline focuses on specific themes or topics that you want to explore in your memoir. It allows you to organize your memories and stories around central ideas, emotions, or lessons you want to convey. For example, if your memoir revolves around themes of resilience and overcoming adversity, you can structure your outline to highlight these aspects.

Event-Based Outline: This type of outline revolves around significant events or milestones in your life. You can identify key moments—such as a career achievement, a personal triumph, or a life-altering experience—and structure your memoir around these events. Each event serves as a chapter or a section in your outline, and you can dive deeper into the impact and meaning of each event as you write.

Geographical Outline: If your memoir involves different locations that play a significant role in your story, you might consider using a geographical outline. This type of outline focuses on the places you have lived, traveled to, or had significant experiences in. It allows you to explore the influence of different environments on your life and provides a unique perspective for structuring your memoir.

Emotional Outline: In an emotional outline, you organize your memoir around the emotional arc you have experienced throughout your life. You can identify and map out the range of emotions you want to convey, such as joy, fear, love, grief, and hope. This outline helps to ensure that the emotional arc of your memoir is well-developed.

Remember, these outlines are just starting points; you can combine or modify them to suit your needs. The most important aspect is to use an outline structure that works best for you and supports the story you want to tell.

To help you understand how these outlines can be implemented, here are some samples:

Chronological Outline:

    I. Childhood:
        a. Early family life
        b. School experiences
        c. Significant friendships
    II. Adolescence:
        a. Coming-of-age moments
        b. Educational pursuits
        c. First romantic relationships
    III. Adulthood:
        a. Career choices and challenges
        b. Personal achievements
        c. Family and relationships
    IV. Present:
        a. Reflections on the past
        b. Lessons learned
        c. Future aspirations

Thematic Outline:

    I. Theme: Resilience
        a. Childhood struggles
        b. Overcoming adversity
        c. Building inner strength

II. Theme: Self-Discovery
   a. Exploring personal identity
   b. Embracing passions and talents
   c. Finding purpose and meaning
III. Theme: Transformation
   a. Life-changing experiences
   b. Growth and personal development
   c. Evolving perspectives

Event-Based Outline:

I. The Career Breakthrough:
   a. Decision to pursue a specific career path
   b. Challenges and obstacles faced
   c. Achieving professional success
II. The Journey Abroad:
   a. Decision to travel or move to a foreign country
   b. Cultural immersion and experiences
   c. Lessons learned and personal growth
III. The Personal Loss:
   a. Coping with grief and loss
   b. Emotional healing and resilience
   c. Finding peace and moving forward

Geographical Outline:

I. Hometown:
   a. Early memories and upbringing
   b. Community influences and connections
   c. Shaping personal values and beliefs

II. City A:
   a. College years and formative experiences
   b. Career beginnings and challenges
   c. Relationships and personal growth
III. City B:
   a. New opportunities and adventures
   b. Cultural experiences and discoveries
   c. Reflections on the impact of the city on personal development

Emotional Outline:

I. Joy:
   a. Childhood innocence and happiness
   b. Moments of triumph and celebration
   c. Finding joy in everyday life
II. Fear:
   a. Confronting fears and overcoming obstacles
   b. Anxiety and uncertainty in challenging times
   c. Strategies for managing fear and embracing courage
III. Love:
   a. Relationships and connections
   b. Love lost and found
   c. Lessons in love and self-discovery

These examples demonstrate how each type of outline focuses on different aspects of a memoir, providing a structure that guides the narrative and ensures a cohesive storytelling experience. Remember to adapt and customize these outlines to fit your own unique memoir.

INDEX CARD ORGANIZING SYSTEM

As far as physically executing these outline options, I prefer the index card system. Index cards provide a flexible and tangible way to organize your thoughts and ideas. Each card represents a specific topic or event in your memoir, allowing you to rearrange and reorganize them easily. You can lay them out on a table, pin them on a board, or shuffle them around until you find the most compelling structure for your narrative.

Index cards also offer a visual representation of your memoir's structure. By physically interacting with the cards and their arrangement, you can gain a better understanding of the flow of your story, identify gaps or repetitive sections, and spot areas where more details or anecdotes might be needed. This visual aspect can enhance your overall planning and writing process.

Writing a memoir can be a daunting task, especially when organizing a vast amount of memories and experiences. Index cards break down your memoir into manageable, bite-sized chunks. Instead of staring at a blank page, you can focus on one specific event or memory at a time. This approach reduces apprehension and allows you to tackle your memoir in a more systematic manner.

The index card system also makes for easy editing and revision. As you progress with your memoir, you may find the need to add, remove, or modify certain sections. Luckily, when using this system, revisions are straightforward. You can easily replace or reposition cards, rewrite information, or add new ideas without disrupting the overall structure. This adaptability makes it easier to refine your memoir and ensure a cohesive narrative.

Lastly, index cards are small and portable, making them convenient for working on your memoir wherever you go.

Whether you're at a coffee shop, on a train, or simply sitting in your backyard, you can easily pull out your index cards and jot down ideas, make notes, or reorganize your story. This accessibility allows for continuous progress and prevents ideas from slipping away. While the index card system may not be suitable for everyone, many writers find it to be a valuable tool for outlining and organizing a memoir.

THEME

So, when we talk "theme," what is that, exactly? Theme is a central idea, message, or concept that runs through a piece of literature. It represents the underlying meaning or insight that the author wants to convey. Themes in memoirs often reflect the author's experiences, emotions, and the overall purpose of their story.

Themes provide a unifying thread that ties the various elements of a memoir together, offering a deeper understanding of the author's experiences and insights. Let's dig into why themes are crucial and how writers can discover and select themes to incorporate into their memoirs.

Themes also play a significant role in memoirs as they provide a lens through which the author's story is explored and interpreted. They are the underlying ideas, messages, or concepts that are woven throughout the narrative, guiding the reader's understanding and allowing for a deeper connection with the author's experiences. Themes give coherence to the memoir by highlighting the central concepts or emotions that drive the story.

Deciding which themes to incorporate in a memoir can be a thoughtful and introspective process for writers.

Here are a few examples of themes commonly found in memoirs:

Resilience: This theme explores the ability to bounce back and recover from adversity or challenges. It focuses on the author's strength, determination, and ability to overcome obstacles in their life. Example: A memoir theme of resilience could be showcased through a writer's account of surviving a life-threatening illness, navigating personal loss, or facing and triumphing over significant hardships.

Identity and Self-Discovery: This theme digs into the author's exploration of their own identity, sense of self, and path toward self-discovery. It often involves introspection, questioning societal norms, and uncovering personal truths. Example: A memoir theme of identity and self-discovery might revolve around a writer's exploration of their cultural heritage, or their personal values and beliefs.

Family and Relationships: This theme focuses on the author's experiences within their familial relationships, friendships, or romantic partnerships. It explores the dynamics, complexities, and impact of these connections on the author's life. Example: A memoir theme of family and relationships could be brought to life through stories of reconciliation with estranged family members, the impact of a significant friendship, or the challenges and growth experienced in a romantic relationship.

Transformation and Growth: This theme highlights the author's personal growth, evolution, and transformative experiences. It often involves pivotal moments, life-changing events, and the lessons learned along the way. Example: A memoir theme of transformation and growth might be depicted through a writer's pursuit of a passion or dream, or their process of healing and finding inner strength.

Loss and Grief: This theme explores the author's experiences of loss, grief, and the process of mourning. It examines the emotional impact, coping mechanisms, and the path toward healing. Example: A memoir theme of loss and grief could be portrayed through the author's account of losing a loved one, navigating personal tragedy, or the emotional aftermath of a significant life event.

These examples illustrate how themes provide a lens through which the memoirist can explore and convey the deeper meaning and insights of their personal experiences. Themes add depth, cohesion, and resonance to memoirs, enriching the reader's understanding and connection with the author's story.

Okay, now let's look at the memories you've written down and the outline you've created and start focusing on your theme.

Take some time to do this. It's a process, and every step is important; there's no rush. Remember to seek feedback as well. Share your stories with beta readers, writing groups, or a writing coach and ask for feedback on the themes they see emerging from your writing. Identifying the theme of your memoir requires careful reflection and analysis. It's important to be open to feedback and willing to revise your manuscript to ensure that the theme is clear and resonant with readers.

Here are some writing prompts that can help you figure out your theme:

Reflect on a period of your life that was particularly transformative or challenging. Write about the lessons you learned during that time and the overall message or insight that emerged from your experiences.

Think about the recurring patterns or events in your life that have had a significant impact. Write about these patterns and explore the underlying themes or messages that connect them.

Imagine yourself giving advice to someone going through a similar experience as the one you want to write about. What key lessons or wisdom would you share? Use this exercise to distill the core theme or themes you want to convey in your memoir.

Consider the relationships that have influenced your life the most. Write about the dynamics, conflicts, and growth that occurred within these relationships. Look for common themes in these interactions that can serve as the foundation for your memoir's theme.

Write about a personal struggle or challenge you faced and how you overcame it. Reflect on the deeper meaning behind your story and the overarching message you want to share with readers.

Think about the values, beliefs, or passions that have guided your life. Write about how these core aspects of your identity have shaped your experiences and choices. Explore the themes that emerge from this exercise.

Consider the societal or cultural issues that have impacted your life. Write about your personal experiences within these contexts and reflect on the larger themes or messages that arise from these encounters.

Write a list of the most significant moments or turning points in your life. Reflect on the emotions, insights, or realizations associated with each event. Look for common threads or themes that run through these moments.

Remember, a theme is the underlying message or insight that runs throughout your memoir. It provides a unifying thread and gives your story depth and resonance. These writing prompts will help you explore your experiences, relationships, values, and challenges to identify the themes that are most meaningful to you.

WORKING WITH LEIF GARRETT

Working with Leif Garrett on his memoir, *Idol Truth*, was a writing experience unlike any other. As we unpacked his early career, we were faced with a significant challenge: how to reveal a never-before-told story that exposed the stark contrast between the image that had been created around him and his true desires as an artist. It was a delicate tightrope walk, as we aimed to shed light on the truth while also capturing the emotional turmoil that Leif experienced during that time.

Leif's early career was built upon a carefully crafted image that positioned him as a teen heartthrob and singer. But behind the scenes, he longed to be recognized as a legitimate artist—a true singer who could pour his heart and soul into his music.

However, his handlers and those around him had different priorities. They were more interested in capitalizing on his popularity and the financial success he could generate.

In our discussions, Leif shared the inner conflict he faced during those years. He expressed his frustration and longing to break free from the confines of his manufactured image. It tortured him to know that his true desires as a singer were not being nurtured or given the attention they deserved. The dichotomy between his personal aspirations and the expectations placed upon him became a source of immense internal struggle.

As we began the task of revealing this untold story, we recognized the importance of not only recounting the facts but also capturing the emotional struggles Leif went through during that period. It was crucial to convey the depth of his yearning for artistic credibility and the pain he experienced as his desires clashed with the commercial interests of those around him.

Writing about these often shocking revelations was not without its challenges. Leif and I understood the inherent risks and fears associated with unveiling such a truth. But we both recognized the necessity of sharing this untold chapter of his life. It was an opportunity for healing and liberation—not just for Leif, but for those who had followed his career and longed to understand the complexities beneath the surface.

Throughout the writing process, we carefully wove together the narrative, intertwining the facts of Leif's life and his emotional experiences. We wanted to honor his truth while also conveying the internal struggles he faced. It was a delicate balancing act, but one that we approached with great sensitivity and respect.

Leif's story serves as a reminder that the path to artistic ful-fillment is not always straightforward. It is a testament to the resilience of the human spirit and the power of self-discovery. By revealing the truth behind his early career, Leif sought to inspire others to embrace their true passions, even in the face of adversity.

As we worked together, Leif and I navigated the difficult terrain of unveiling his hidden truth. We confronted the fears and uncertainties head-on, acknowledging the weight of the revelations while ensuring that his emotional arc remained at the forefront. It was a collaborative effort that required trust, empathy, and a shared commitment to capturing the essence of his experience. In the end, Leif's memoir became a testament to his courage. It revealed the depths of his torment and the strength it took to navigate a world that often prioritized image over artistry. Through his story, he not only shed light on a hid-den chapter of his life but also offered solace and understanding to those who have faced similar struggles.

By sharing his truth, Leif aimed to shed light on his own story and to inspire others who may be grappling with simi-lar challenges. He wanted to remind them that it's okay to acknowledge the pain, the conflicts, and the desires that may deviate from the expectations imposed upon them. Through his vulnerability, he offered solace and hope to those who have felt the weight of their own unspoken truths.

Writing Leif's memoir was a transformative experience for both of us. It allowed us to dig into the depths of his emotions, to navigate the complexities of his past, and ultimately, to find healing. Our collaboration became one of self-discovery, push-ing the boundaries of storytelling.

CHAPTER 12

Narrative Arcs and Structure

I'd next like to discuss another fundamental element of memoir writing: the narrative arc. Simply put, narrative arc refers to the flow of your memoir. In other words, it's the way you organize and present your story. The structure. It's like a roadmap that guides your readers through the events and experiences of your life. Imagine your memoir as a journey—an adventure through your past, your memories, and your personal growth. The narrative arc is what gives shape and direction to that journey. It's like walking along a path, step by step, as you recount the significant moments and reflections that have shaped you.

In a memoir with a linear narrative arc, the path is straightforward and follows a chronological order. It's like taking a stroll along a straight road, starting from the beginning and moving forward in time until you reach the end of your story. You don't skip ahead or jump back; you allow your readers to experience your life events as they unfolded. By using a linear narrative arc, you create a sense of coherence and clarity. Your readers can easily connect the dots, understand cause and effect, and witness the growth and transformation you experienced over time. It's like building a solid foundation for your memoir, one brick at a time. Your memoir is not just a collection of random memories. It's a story with a purpose—a story that invites your readers to join you in your story. By employing a linear narrative arc, you provide them with a clear path to follow, ensuring they stay connected and invested in your experiences.

Angela's Ashes is Frank McCourt's memoir about his childhood growing up in poverty in Limerick, Ireland. The memoir is structured chronologically, following McCourt's life from his birth to his early adulthood.

The memoir begins with McCourt's birth in Brooklyn, New York, and follows his family's return to Ireland, where they struggle to make ends meet. McCourt describes the harsh conditions he and his siblings face, including hunger, illness, and the death of several family members. As the memoir progresses, McCourt attends school and navigates the challenges of adolescence, including his first romantic relationships and his struggle to find his place in the world. He also reflects on the role of religion in his life, as he attends Catholic school and grapples with his own doubts and questions.

At the end of the memoir, McCourt leaves Ireland to start a new life in America. He reflects on the lessons he has learned during his difficult childhood and looks forward to a brighter future.

By using a chronological structure, McCourt is able to create a clear and cohesive narrative that follows the trajectory of his life. This structure allows us to understand the context of his experiences and how they shaped him into the person he became. It also allows the reader to witness McCourt's growth and development over time.

That said, as effective and relied-upon as the linear narrative arc is, there are other narrative arc options. I'll describe several more below.

Circular narrative arc: A circular narrative arc loops back to the beginning of the story, often to show the growth or change that the author has undergone since the beginning. This type of arc can be particularly effective in memoirs that explore themes of transformation or self-discovery.

In *Inheritance*, Dani Shapiro explores the shocking discovery that her father was not her biological parent. The memoir opens with Shapiro's recollection of taking a DNA test on a whim and receiving unexpected results. From there, Shapiro goes back to the beginning of her life, exploring her childhood and relationship with her father, who was an Orthodox Jew.

Throughout the memoir, Shapiro grapples with the questions raised by her discovery: Who is she? Where does she come from? As she unpacks her family's history, she uncovers secrets and hidden truths, piecing together a new understanding of her identity.

At the end of her memoir, Shapiro returns to the present day, reflecting on the ways that her discovery has changed her. She realizes that the truth of her biological identity is only a small part of the story, and what really matters is the relationships she has built with the people she loves. By circling back to the beginning of the story, Shapiro illustrates how her discovery has transformed her understanding of her past and her present, and how it has led her to a deeper appreciation of the people and experiences that have shaped her life.

Thematic narrative arc: Rather than following a strict timeline, a memoir can be structured around themes or topics that the author wants to explore. This approach allows the author to focus on specific experiences or ideas and tie them together thematically.

A thematic arc is a narrative structure that organizes a story around a particular theme or set of themes. In a memoir, this can be an effective way to explore a particular topic or idea in depth. For example, in the memoir *Wild* by Cheryl Strayed, the central theme is the author's journey of self-discovery and healing as she hikes the Pacific Crest Trail. Throughout the book, Strayed weaves together different experiences and memories that reflect this theme, such as her struggles with addiction, her relationship with her mother, and her experiences on the trail itself.

By using a thematic arc, Strayed is able to explore the deeper meaning and significance of her journey, and to reflect on the ways in which it has transformed her as a person. She is also able to draw connections between seemingly disparate events and experiences, creating a more nuanced and complex portrait of herself.

A thematic narrative arc can be a powerful tool, allowing the author to explore complex themes and ideas in a way that is insightful and emotionally resonant.

Braided narrative arc: In a braided arc, the author weaves together multiple timelines or themes to create a cohesive narrative. This approach can be particularly effective when there are multiple storylines or ideas that the author wants to explore.

The braided arc is a narrative technique that weaves together multiple threads in a memoir. This technique allows the writer to explore different facets of their life and experiences in a non-linear way, creating a richer and more complex story.

To create a braided arc in a memoir, the writer should identify the different strands of their story, such as different time periods, relationships, or themes. These strands are then woven together in a way that creates an interconnected and meaningful narrative.

For example, a memoir about a person's life might braid together the stories of their childhood, their career, and their family relationships. The writer might alternate between these different strands, using transitions and connections to tie them together thematically.

While the braided arc can be a powerful tool for exploring the complexity of a person's life and experiences, it can also be challenging to execute effectively. To create a successful braided structure, you should consider the following tips:

Choose the right strands: The different strands of your story should be meaningful and complementary, rather than arbitrary or disconnected.

Use clear transitions: The writer should use clear transitions between different strands to help the reader follow the narrative.

Connect the strands thematically: The different strands should be connected in a way that creates a cohesive and meaningful whole.

Be mindful of pacing: The braided structure can be slower-paced than a linear narrative, so the writer should be mindful of pacing to keep readers engaged.

Use repetition and callbacks: The writer can use repetition and callbacks to tie the different strands together and create a sense of coherence.

Here's an example of how the braided narrative arc can be used in memoir:

In *The Color of Water* by James McBride, the author tells the story of his mother, Ruth, and her experiences growing up in a Jewish family in the South during the early twentieth century. The author also writes about his own experiences growing up as a Black man in New York City during the 1960s and 1970s. The two narratives are interwoven throughout the book, creating a complex and layered story that explores issues of race, identity, and family.

The chapters alternate between Ruth's story and McBride's story, with each chapter building on the themes and experiences explored in the previous chapter. Ruth's story explores her difficult upbringing as the daughter of a rabbi, her eventual marriage to a Black man, and her struggles to raise her children as both Jewish and Black. McBride's story explores his experiences growing up in poverty in New York City, his struggles with his identity as a Black man with a white mother, and his eventual reconciliation with his mother's past.

The braided arc in *The Color of Water* allows McBride to explore complex issues of race and identity from multiple perspectives, creating a rich and nuanced story that is both personal and universal. The interweaving of Ruth's story and McBride's story creates a sense of connection and continuity, highlighting the ways in which the past shapes the present and the future. The braided structure in *The Color of Water* is a powerful technique that allows the author to explore complex themes and ideas in a creative way.

The braided arc is a fantastic way to create a rich and nuanced memoir, but it requires careful planning and execution to be effective.

Circular structure: A memoir can also be structured in a circular or cyclical way, where the story starts and ends in the same place or with the same event. This approach can be particularly effective for memoirs that focus on personal growth or transformation.

A circular structure in memoir is a narrative technique that creates a sense of completion and resolution. This type of structure can be particularly effective in memoir because it allows the writer to explore their experiences in a nonlinear way—while still providing a sense of closure.

To create a circular structure in a memoir, the writer should identify the key themes and experiences they want to explore, as well as the starting and ending points of the story. The memoir can then be structured around a series of events or experiences that include these themes, leading back to the starting point at the end of the story.

For example, a memoir might begin with the writer's arrival in a new city and end with their departure, with the story exploring the experiences and relationships they had during their time there.

The circular structure can be a powerful tool for creating a sense of coherence and meaning in a memoir. To create a successful circular structure, the writer should consider the following tips:

186

Choose a clear starting and ending point: The starting and ending points of the story should be meaningful and clear, creating a sense of completion and resolution.

Use clear transitions: The writer should use clear transitions between different parts of the story to help the reader follow the narrative.

Connect the experiences thematically: The different experiences in the story should be connected thematically, creating a cohesive and meaningful whole.

Use repetition and callbacks: The writer can use repetition and callbacks to tie the different parts of the story together and create a sense of coherence.

Be mindful of pacing: The circular structure can be slower-paced than a linear narrative, so the writer should be mindful of pacing and keep readers engaged.

Here's an example of a memoir with a circular structure:

In *The Glass Castle* by Jeannette Walls, the author uses a circular structure to weave together her memories of growing up in poverty with her dysfunctional family. The memoir begins and ends with a scene of the author's mother, Rose Mary, rummaging through a dumpster in New York City. This opening and closing scene serves as a metaphor for the author's journey to come to terms with her upbringing and the role her parents played in her life.

Throughout the memoir, Walls moves back and forth in time, exploring different aspects of her childhood and her relationship with her parents. However, she always returns to the opening scene of her mother in the dumpster, showing how her past continues to shape her present. By using this circular structure, Walls creates a powerful sense of closure at the end of the memoir, as she reflects on how her experiences have made her who she is today.

The circular structure is a powerful technique for creating a sense of completion and resolution in a memoir.

Fragmented narrative arc: A fragmented narrative arc jumps around in time, presenting events and memories out of chronological order. This type of arc can be used to convey a sense of confusion or disorientation, or to highlight certain themes or motifs.

Wasted: A Memoir of Anorexia and Bulimia by Marya Hornbacher is about the author's battle with anorexia and bulimia. The memoir is structured as a series of fragmented memories, with Hornbacher jumping back and forth in time as she recounts her experiences.

Hornbacher's memories are vivid and visceral, evoking the physical and emotional pain of her illness. She recounts her obsession with food and her compulsive behaviors around eating and purging. She also examines the underlying psychological and emotional issues that contributed to her illness, including trauma, anxiety, and a deep sense of self-loathing.

As the memoir progresses, Hornbacher's memories become more disjointed and fragmented, reflecting the disorientation and confusion of her illness. She explores the ways that anorexia and bulimia warped her sense of self, making it difficult for her to distinguish reality from fantasy.

Episodic narrative arc: An episodic narrative arc consists of a series of self-contained episodes or vignettes, often loosely connected by a common theme or setting. This type of arc can be used to create a collage-like portrait of the author's life, or to explore different aspects of their personality or identity.

Me Talk Pretty One Day is David Sedaris's memoir about his experiences living in France and learning to speak French. The memoir is structured as a series of loosely connected essays, each of which explores a different aspect of Sedaris's life in France.

In one essay, Sedaris recounts the difficulties he faces trying to communicate with his French teacher, who is strict and unyielding. In another essay, he describes the bizarre and surreal experience of attending a French language class with a group of eccentric students.

Throughout the memoir, Sedaris offers witty observations and humorous anecdotes about French culture and language. He reflects on his own experiences as a language learner and the challenges of adapting to a new culture.

At the end of the memoir, Sedaris reflects on the ways his experiences in France have shaped him, including the lessons he has learned about language, culture, and communication. By using an episodic narrative arc, Sedaris creates a sense of playfulness and unpredictability that captures the humor and absurdity of his experiences in France. This type of narrative arc allows the reader to dip in and out of his life, exploring different facets of his experience without being tied to a single plot or thread.

Quest narrative arc: A quest narrative arc follows the author's journey to achieve a particular goal or fulfill a particular purpose. This type of arc can be particularly effective in memoirs that explore themes of personal growth or spiritual awakening.

Wild: From Lost to Found on the Pacific Crest Trail is Cheryl Strayed's memoir about her 1,100-mile hike on the Pacific Crest Trail. The memoir is structured as a quest narrative, with Strayed setting out on her trip as a way to escape the pain and grief of her past and find a sense of purpose and direction in her life.

As Strayed hikes the trail, she faces a series of physical and emotional challenges. She struggles to carry the heavy backpack that contains all of her supplies and navigates treacherous terrain and dangerous wildlife. Along the way, she reflects on the events that led her to undertake this journey, including the death of her mother and the dissolution of her marriage.

Throughout the memoir, Strayed meets a variety of other hikers and encounters moments of unexpected kindness and generosity. She also confronts her own limitations and fears, pushing herself to complete the trail despite the odds against her.

At the end of the memoir, Strayed reaches the end of the Pacific Crest Trail and reflects on the lessons she has learned. She realizes that, while the hike was physically challenging, it was also a transformative experience that helped her confront her past and find a sense of purpose and direction for her future. By using a quest narrative arc, Strayed emphasizes the transformative nature of her journey and the ways in which it helped her achieve a deeper understanding of herself and the world around her.

Ultimately, the narrative arc chosen for a memoir depends on the author's intentions, the story they want to tell, and the themes they want to explore. Each of these arcs can be used to create a compelling and meaningful memoir.

A JOHN CHEEVER MEMORY

Accompanying John Cheever to Sing Sing prison to read selections from his book *Falconer* was a remarkable and memorable experience. At the age of sixteen or so, I recall the heightened security measures we encountered as we made our way through the prison gates. The formidable walls and fences served as a constant reminder of the confined environment we were about to enter.

Once inside, we were greeted by prison officials who guided us through the complex, navigating a maze of corridors and checkpoints. The atmosphere was tense—as one would expect in a maximum-security facility—but there was also an air of anticipation mixed with curiosity. It was evident that Cheever's presence was significant to both the prisoners and the staff.

As we reached the designated area, we were met by a group of inmates, numbering a couple of dozen, who were seated and respectfully awaiting the reading. Their demeanor was strikingly different from the audience at the Ossining Public Library, which I had witnessed firsthand a few weeks prior. Here, in this confined space, the audience seemed more engaged, more receptive to Cheever's words. It was as if they found solace and connection in the themes explored in *Falconer*, which explores the human condition, introspection, and redemption.

Cheever, too, appeared to be genuinely at ease in this setting. He spoke with conviction, his words resonating deeply with the captive audience. It was evident that he related to them on a deeply personal level, recognizing the shared struggles and experiences that transcend societal boundaries. There was a rawness to his interactions, as if he felt a kinship with these individuals who hailed from a different world.

The prisoners listened intently, hanging on his every word, and eagerly posed questions that showcased their appreciation for his work. The exchange felt meaningful, like a bridge momentarily connecting two distinct worlds. In those moments, the confines of the prison walls faded away, and a genuine human connection was forged through the power of literature.

Looking back on that experience, I realized that it offered a glimpse into a side of Cheever that was perhaps less visible in other settings. In Sing Sing, he seemed to shed any pretense or social barriers, allowing his true self to emerge. It was a testament to the transformative power of art and our ability as humans to find common ground even in the most unlikely of circumstances.

It was so interesting to observe the contrasting dynamics between Cheever's interactions with the audience at the public library and the prisoners at Sing Sing. While Cheever may have appeared somewhat aloof or detached when receiving praise at the public library, his demeanor shifted noticeably within the prison environment.

In the prison setting, Cheever seemed to shed any inhibitions or distance, actively engaging with the prisoners by asking questions and genuinely listening to their responses. This shift in behavior could be attributed to a variety of factors. First, the prisoners themselves may have elicited a different response from Cheever compared to the general public. Their circumstances, experiences, and struggles may have resonated with him on a deeper level, fostering a stronger sense of empathy and connection.

Additionally, the nature of the prison reading may have encouraged a more interactive dynamic. The prisoners, being confined and seeking solace or redemption, may have been more inclined to actively participate in the discussion. Their questions and responses might have provided Cheever with a unique opportunity to engage in meaningful dialogue, exploring the themes of his work in a more profound manner.

Maybe the prison environment itself—with its heightened sense of reality and the stark contrast between freedom and confinement—contributed to a more authentic and open interaction. The stripped-down nature of the prison setting may have allowed Cheever to let his guard down and connect with the prisoners on a more genuine level. The difference in Cheever's engagement between the public library and the prison highlights the complex interplay between the author, the audience, and the environment. I found it all riveting—the power context and personal connection has in shaping interpersonal dynamics, and the way individuals relate to one another.

CHAPTER 13

Dialogue, Character Development, and Scene Building

I believe that eavesdropping is, to some extent, ingrained in our human nature. Think about it: when we stumble upon an intriguing conversation, who among us can resist the temptation to tune in and catch every word? It's almost instinctual. And you know what? I think incorporating dialogue into our memoirs shares that same captivating quality. It presents us with an opportunity to offer the audience a conversation that is genuinely worth listening to.

Dialogue serves as a powerful tool to propel the story forward. It breathes life into the narrative, allowing it to flow naturally and effortlessly. It's an avenue for characters to reveal crucial details, providing readers with a more personal and immersive experience of the story's unfolding action. Through dialogue, we engage in a form of "show, don't tell" writing, where the characters' words become vehicles for painting memorable images and evoking emotions.

Dialogue also serves another purpose: to break up long blocks of text. As you flip through the pages of a book, encountering a well-placed conversation allows your eyes and brain to take a momentary breather. Dialogue offers the reader a chance to relax and absorb the information in a more digestible manner.

However, it's essential to remember that dialogue should never exist merely for the sake of conversation. It must have a purpose—a dual purpose, in fact. It should reveal something about the characters or the story while simultaneously driving the narrative forward. Each line spoken should contribute to the larger tapestry of the memoir, weaving together a rich and compelling tale.

When crafting your stories, embrace the power of dialogue. Use it as a means to captivate your audience, to grant them a front-row seat to conversations that matter. Let it be the driving force behind your narrative, while also offering a respite for weary eyes. But above all, ensure that every spoken word serves a purpose—one that enlightens your story toward its ultimate destination.

WHAT ELSE DOES DIALOGUE DO?

When dialogue is skillfully interspersed throughout the narrative, it creates a rhythm that draws readers deeper into the story. It provides a natural flow, guiding them through the pages with a sense of anticipation. The interplay of voices, the back-and-forth exchanges, and the subtleties of conversation create a captivating tapestry that engages the reader's imagination.

Dialogue possesses a unique power to reveal the nuances of characters and relationships. It unveils their idiosyncrasies, quirks, and distinct voices, allowing readers to forge a deeper connection with the individuals portrayed. Through dialogue, readers gain insight into the emotions, motivations, and conflicts that shape the narrative. It is through these conversations that characters truly come alive, becoming more than mere figures on the page.

In memoir, dialogue also serves as a bridge to the past. It allows you to recreate conversations that took place years, even decades, ago. By reconstructing these dialogues, writers can transport readers back in time, immersing them in the events and emotions of the past. It is a powerful tool for recapturing the essence of significant moments and encounters, ensuring that they remain vivid and tangible.

By incorporating dialogue, authors bring their stories to life, allowing readers to engage more intimately with the experiences and characters being portrayed. Here are some other key reasons why dialogue is important in this genre:

Authenticity and Realism: Dialogue adds an element of realism to memoirs and first-person narrative nonfiction. It recreates the actual words spoken by individuals, capturing their unique voices, mannerisms, and idiosyncrasies. By presenting conversations as they occurred, writers make the reader feel like they are witnessing the events firsthand. And if you're concerned about recounting dialogue as 100 percent accurate, remember, unless it was recorded it's almost impossible to do that. Recount it to the best of your memory, as there is some creative license with this. Capture the spirit of the conversation. Bottom line, authors should strive for accuracy and ethical representation when reconstructing conversations from memory, ensuring that dialogue remains true to the essence of the original events.

Character Development: Dialogue is a powerful tool for character development. It reveals the personalities, perspectives, and emotions of individuals involved in the story. Through their words, readers gain insights into the characters' thoughts, motivations, and relationships. The unique ways in which characters express themselves through dialogue can deepen understanding and empathy for them.

Emotion and Tension: Dialogue brings emotions to life. It allows writers to convey the intensity, subtleties, and complexities of human interactions. Through conversations, authors can explore the emotional dynamics between characters and reveal conflicts, desires, and more. By incorporating tension and conflict into dialogue, the narrative becomes more compelling, holding the reader's attention and creating a sense of anticipation.

Scene Setting and Description: Dialogue can serve as a vehicle for scene setting and description, complementing the author's exposition. Instead of relying solely on descriptive passages, authors can use dialogue to reveal details about the setting, time, and place. By intertwining dialogue with descriptions, writers create a more immersive experience.

Voice and Language: Dialogue allows authors to showcase the unique voices and linguistic styles of the individuals involved. Each character's way of speaking can reflect their background, education, social class, and personality traits. By carefully crafting dialogue, authors can create distinct voices, enhancing the richness and diversity of their narratives.

Narrative Pacing: Well-placed dialogue can enhance the pacing of a memoir or first-person narrative nonfiction. It breaks up lengthy prose, injecting energy and movement into the story. Dialogue creates a natural rhythm, propelling the narrative forward and preventing it from becoming monotonous. Dialogue can also be used strategically to slow down the pace during important or emotionally charged moments.

Remember that, while dialogue is a valuable tool, it should be used judiciously. You must strike a balance between dialogue and other narrative elements to avoid overwhelming the reader or diluting the impact of the story.

Here are the basic kinds of dialogue—both direct and indirect—that you can consider incorporating into your memoir:

1. **Direct Dialogue**: Direct dialogue involves presenting conversations between characters exactly as they occur, using quotation marks to indicate the spoken words. It is the most common form of dialogue in storytelling. Direct dialogue allows readers to experience the conversation firsthand and provides a sense of immediacy. It is effective for capturing important moments, interactions, and conversations that are crucial to your memoir.

   Examples:

   "I can't believe we're finally here!" Laura exclaimed.

"I'm sorry," she whispered, her voice
barely audible.

"I won't let you down," he promised,
determination in his eyes.

"What's your favorite book?" she asked
with genuine curiosity.

"I can't believe you did that!" he exclaimed,
his face turning red with anger.

"I love you," he said softly, his voice filled
with tenderness.

2. **Indirect Dialogue**: Indirect dialogue, also known as reported speech or indirect speech, involves summarizing or paraphrasing conversations. Instead of presenting the conversation word for word, the writer provides a concise summary or description of what was said. Indirect dialogue is useful for condensing lengthy conversations or conveying the essence of a conversation without going into detail.

Examples:

Laura expressed her excitement about their arrival.

She apologized quietly, her words barely audible.

He assured her that he would not disappoint.

She asked him about his favorite book, genuinely curious.

He expressed his disbelief, his face turning red with anger.

He conveyed his love for her in a soft, tender tone.

3. **Inner Dialogue or Internal Monologue**: Inner dialogue refers to the thoughts, reflections, and emotions of the narrator or protagonist. It allows readers to gain insight into the character's feelings, motivations, and personal growth. Inner dialogue can be presented in both direct and indirect forms, depending on the style and context of your memoir.

Examples:

I was overwhelmed with a sense of accomplishment as years of hard work finally paid off.

As I stood at the crossroads of my life, I couldn't help but wonder if I was making the right choice. What if I regretted it later? But deep down, I knew that I had to follow my heart, even if it meant stepping into the unknown.

The day she left, I felt like my world had crumbled. I replayed our last conversation in my mind, searching for clues, for something I might have missed. Did I say the right things? Could I have done more to make her stay?

I battled with self-doubt every day, questioning my worth and my abilities. It was an uphill climb, but I refused to let my insecurities define me. I had to find the strength to silence the voices of negativity and embrace my true potential.

4. **Nonverbal Dialogue**: Not all communication occurs through spoken words. Nonverbal dialogue includes gestures, facial expressions, body language, and actions that convey meaning. Incorporating nonverbal dialogue into your memoir can add depth and subtlety to character interactions, revealing emotions and enhancing the reader's understanding.

Examples:

Tears welled up in her eyes as she hugged him tightly, conveying her deep gratitude.

I held her hand tightly, finding solace in the warmth of her touch.

His eyes met mine, and in that moment, we understood each other without saying a word.

The old oak tree stood as a silent witness to the memories etched into its weathered bark.

With a simple nod, she reassured me that everything would be okay.

The familiar scent of home enveloped me, evoking memories of a simpler time.

5. **Dialogue Tags**: Lastly, while not a style of dialog per se, dialogue tags are tools of direct dialogue; they are the phrases or words that attribute speech to a specific character. They help clarify who is speaking and add variety to your writing. Common dialogue tags include "said," "asked," "replied," "whispered," and "shouted." When using dialogue tags, it's generally best to keep them simple and unobtrusive.

Examples:

"I can't wait to start this new chapter," John said.

"I can't believe you did that," she said, her eyes filled with concern.

"It was a difficult decision," he explained, his voice tinged with regret.

"You'll always be in my heart," Mom whispered, her voice trembling with emotion.

"I knew I had to take a leap of faith," I admitted, my voice barely above a whisper.

"I'll never forget that moment," he recalled, a wistful smile playing on his lips.

When incorporating dialogue into your memoir, it's crucial to be authentic and true to the people and situations you're portraying. Use dialogue to advance the narrative, reveal character traits, and create scenes that immerse your readers.

Remember that direct dialogue presents the actual words spoken by the characters, while indirect dialogue provides a summary or paraphrase of the conversation. Both forms have their uses, and you can choose which one best suits the context and flow of your story.

Also remember that keeping dialogue short and to the point is important for several reasons:

Realism: In real-life conversations, people generally don't engage in long, uninterrupted monologues. Dialogue that is succinct and concise reflects the natural flow of conversation and feels more authentic to readers.

Pace and Tension: Shorter dialogue helps maintain an appropriate pace in your memoir. It keeps the story moving forward and avoids unnecessary digressions or lengthy explanations. Crisp dialogue can also create tension and suspense, especially in intense or emotional scenes.

Reader Engagement: Long, meandering dialogue can be overwhelming and might cause readers to lose interest or become confused. Clear, concise dialogue keeps readers engaged and focused on the essential aspects of the conversation.

Characterization: The way characters speak can reveal a lot about their personalities, attitudes, and emotions. By using concise dialogue, you can highlight character traits effectively and make each character's voice distinct. This allows readers to grasp the essence of a character's speech patterns, vocabulary, and style.

Avoiding Information Overload: Dialogue should serve a purpose in your memoir, such as advancing the plot, revealing character dynamics, or providing key information. By keeping dialogue focused and concise, you avoid overwhelming readers with excessive details or unnecessary information.

Know that brevity doesn't mean sacrificing depth or impact. Even short snippets of dialogue can convey emotional depth, reveal conflict, or illuminate important aspects of your memoir. Strive to make every word count and ensure that your dialogue contributes meaningfully to the overall narrative.

By using dialogue, you can create a sense of intimacy and immediacy, and bring your experiences and the people around you to life on the page. It's important to use dialogue in a way that feels authentic to your voice and your experiences, and to ensure that your conversations are relevant to the narrative and help move the story forward.

CHARACTER DEVELOPMENT

You are the main character of your memoir, but other people play important roles in the story. You need to learn how to develop the people in your stories, including family members, friends, and other important figures.

When it comes to developing characters, there are several techniques that can be used to bring real people to life on the page:

1. It's important to provide detailed descriptions of the people in the memoir. This can include physical charac-

teristics, mannerisms, and behaviors that help to paint a clear picture of who the person is.

2. Sharing specific anecdotes about the people in the writer's life can help bring them to life on the page. These anecdotes can be funny, poignant, or even tragic, but they should all serve to reveal something about the character.

3. Dialogue is an effective way to show people what a character is like. By including snippets of conversation, the writer can reveal the character's personality, tone, and mannerisms.

4. In memoir writing, it's important to consider the motivations of the people in the writer's life. Why did they act the way they did? What were their goals and desires? By exploring these questions, the writer can develop a deeper understanding of the character and convey this understanding.

5. Nobody is perfect, and by showing the flaws and imperfections of the people in the writer's life, the writer can create more nuanced and complex characters that feel real and relatable.

Developing characters requires a combination of observation, introspection, and empathy. By paying attention to the people in our lives and taking the time to understand them, we can create accurate depictions of them on the page. Consider the character's arc in your memoir. How does the character change over the course of the story? What events or experiences contribute to this change? Reflect on the character's experiences and what you want the reader to take away from it. What themes or lessons emerge from the character's story? How does the character's journey contribute to the overall message of your memoir?

Here is a character description I wrote:

> As I walked into the crowded cafeteria, I saw her sitting alone at a table in the corner. She was a tall, thin woman with short, curly hair that was dyed a bright shade of red. Her eyes were a piercing blue, and she wore a pair of large, round glasses that magnified them even more. Despite her thin frame, she had a commanding presence that made her stand out in a crowd.

> As I approached her table, she looked up and smiled at me warmly. "Hey there!" she said, her voice deep and melodious. "I'm so glad you could make it."

> I sat down across from her and took a closer look at her appearance. She was wearing a long, flowing skirt that swirled around her legs as she moved, and a loose-fitting blouse that was studded with colorful beads. Her hands were adorned with stacks of silver rings, and she wore a pendant necklace that looked like it had been handcrafted.

> As we began to talk, I noticed that her personality was just as unique as her appearance. She was confident and self-assured, with a quick wit and a sharp tongue. She had a way of making me feel at ease, even though we had just met, and I found myself opening up to her in ways that I never had before.

Through her words and actions, I could tell that she was a free spirit who marched to the beat of her own drum. She was passionate about art and literature, and loved nothing more than getting lost in a good book or exploring a new art exhibit. She was also fiercely independent and didn't care much for social conventions or the opinions of others.

This character description uses a combination of physical details and personality traits to create a memorable image of the character. By focusing on unique details—such as the character's dyed hair, large glasses, and handcrafted jewelry—the description helps the character come to life in the reader's mind. Additionally, by highlighting the character's personality traits—such as her confidence, wit, and passion for art—the description gives us a sense of who the character is and what makes her unique.

Try this: choose a character from your memoir. This can be yourself, a family member, a friend, or anyone else who plays a significant role in your story. Write a character sketch of this person, describing their personality, traits, and behaviors. Use sensory details to help the reader visualize the character and get a sense of who they are as a person.

SCENE BUILDING

Scene building is a crucial aspect of writing a compelling memoir. When you create a strong scene, it provides an immersive experience for your readers, allowing them to connect with your story on a deeper level. Dialogue plays a significant role within these scenes, as it brings your characters to life and adds a dynamic element to the narrative.

Building a scene requires attention to detail and a focus on the sensory experience. A well-crafted scene can bring us into the world of the memoir and create a sense of immersion. Here are some tips for building a scene:

Start with a strong opening sentence: The opening sentence of a scene should grab our attention and set the stage for what's to come. It should create a sense of intrigue or anticipation and draw the reader in.

Use powerful descriptions: In order to create a sense of immersion, it's important to use powerful descriptions that engage the senses. Describe the sights, sounds, smells, and tactile sensations of the scene, and use sensory language to create a rich and detailed picture in the reader's mind.

Include dialogue: Dialogue can help bring a scene to life and create a sense of tension or conflict. Use dialogue to reveal character traits, advance the plot, and add depth to the scene.

Pay attention to pacing: A scene should have a natural ebb and flow, with moments of tension and release. Pay attention to the pacing of the scene and use sentence structure and word choice to create a sense of momentum or to slow things down.

Use your own perspective: Memoir writing is unique in that it's based on the writer's own experiences. Use your own perspective to add depth and nuance to the scene, and to create a sense of emotional resonance.

Building a scene requires attention to detail, a focus on sensory experience, the inclusion of dialogue, intentional pacing, and the use of the writer's own perspective. By following these tips, memoir writers can create scenes that are immersive and emotionally resonant.

Here is an exercise that can help you build scenes in your memoir:

Choose a significant event from your life that you want to include in your memoir. It could be a moment of triumph, a moment of loss, or a moment of personal growth. Imagine yourself back in that moment and focus on the details. What did you see, hear, smell, taste, and feel? What was the weather like? What were the surroundings? Write down as many details as you can remember.

Use sensory language to bring the scene to life. Instead of saying, "I was scared," describe the physical sensations you felt. For example, "My heart raced, and my palms were slick with sweat." Use sensory language to describe the sights, sounds, smells, tastes, and physical sensations that you experienced.

Create a timeline of events leading up to the significant moment. Include what you were doing before the event, what happened during the event, and what happened after the event.

Show, don't tell. Instead of telling readers how you felt, show them through your actions and reactions. For example, if you were scared, describe how you reacted. Did you freeze up? Did you run away? Did you scream?

Once you have written the scene, edit and refine it. Cut out any unnecessary details and make sure the scene flows smoothly. Confirm that you've included enough sensory details to bring the scene to life.

Remember, scene building takes practice. It may take time to develop this skill. Keep practicing and experimenting until you find the style that works best for you.

PRE-WRITING

There's a writing technique commonly known as "pre-writing" or "preparatory writing." It involves writing a scene or situation that won't be included in the final story or memoir, but serves as a warm-up or background for the dialogue or scene that will be used. This technique allows the writer to establish momentum, get into the mindset of the characters, and create more authentic dialogue. Here's an example to illustrate this technique:

Example:

Pre-Writing Scene (not included in the memoir):

Joanna sat alone in her childhood bedroom, surrounded by dusty memories and faded photographs. She traced her finger over an old picture of her father, her heart aching with the weight of their past. The bitter argument they had last week still lingered in her mind, the words echoing in her ears as she struggled to understand his point of view. She took a deep breath, determined to find a way to bridge the gap between them.

Memoir Dialogue Scene:

Joanna entered her father's study, her heart pounding in her chest. She found him sitting at his desk, engrossed in his work. Summoning her courage, she cleared her throat and spoke softly, "Dad, can we talk? I've been thinking about what you said the other day, and I want you to know that I understand now. I realize that we've both made mistakes, but I don't want our relationship to suffer because of them. Can we find a way to move forward?"

In this example, the pre-writing scene helps set the emotional groundwork for the dialogue between Joanna and her father. By writing the previous scene, the writer can tap into the character's thoughts, feelings, and motivations, which then inform the depth of the dialogue that follows.

WORKING WITH SHIRLEY BABASHOFF

One afternoon, when renowned Olympian Shirley Babashoff and I were about halfway through working together on her memoir, she looked at me seriously and said, "I don't think we can finish this book."

I didn't know what to say. We had a deadline for the manuscript, had been paid part of an advance, and absolutely *had* to finish the book. But I could see in her eyes that this was something serious. So I turned off the recorder, put everything aside, and asked her to let me know what was on her mind. In an uncharacteristically fragile voice, she began describing the earliest moments of her life, which—like most of us—went back to about two years of age. Then, she described in harrowing detail how she had been sexually abused by her father.

Starting at that age and continuing until she was about thirteen years old, she laid out the brutal details. She had finally fought him off as a teenager because she was finally strong enough to defend herself. Sadly, she had a two-year-old sister her father likely abused once he realized Shirley was capable of fighting back.

We didn't know what to do at this point. I understood what Shirley was saying, and knew this was a huge part of her life. In writing a memoir, you have to be able to tell the truth. But how much truth? Are there limits? How do we deal with it?

This was a first for me, as I had never had a memoir subject bring something up in the middle of the project that was so monumental, it could force us to stop the project. But then we talked more about it in detail, and Shirley began describing how she would stay late at the pool to avoid her father. The pool was her sanctuary, her safety zone. She would get up early and go to the pool to avoid him because he couldn't get to her while she was in the pool. His abuse was forcing her to swim more than she would normally.

The more we talked about it, the more it became evident to me that we had to figure out a way to work it into the story. In a humane way, of course, without being too graphic—but we needed to illustrate just what she had gone through and how it affected her life and her swimming. I stressed to her, "This makes you even more heroic than you already are... And believe me, you are already very heroic."

With that, we began the process of figuring out just how much detail to include about this torturous part of her life. In the end, we provided just enough detail to illustrate the fact that she wasn't just a great swimmer and a born-to-be champion; she was also an incredibly resilient, focused, and strong young woman who somehow managed to stay focused on her Olympic goals. This is the sort of truth that makes her memoir, *Making Waves*, extra special. It's a peek into her life—which she had never shared before—that casts a huge shadow across what she wound up doing as an Olympic champion.

Sometimes the most painful things you've gone through, the things you never thought you would share with anybody, actually play a part in your story. Painful obstacles reveal something about your inner strength, which serves as an inspiration to your readers.

CHAPTER 14

Literary Devices

Literary devices are techniques that writers use to convey meaning, enhance the effectiveness of their writing, and engage readers on an emotional and intellectual level. While memoirs are primarily nonfiction narratives based on real-life experiences, authors often employ literary devices to craft their stories and make them more compelling. There are several literary devices that can be effective when writing a memoir. Some of the most commonly used literary devices include:

IMAGERY

Using strong sensory details and descriptions can transport the reader into the story. Imagery is a powerful tool that can help bring your experiences to life and create an unforgettable, immersive reading experience for your audience. Here are some examples of using imagery in writing memoir:

> "The sun dipped below the horizon, painting the sky with fiery hues of red and orange." This imagery creates a sense of warmth and beauty and could be used to describe a particular moment or event in the memoir. (Often, sunsets are connected to things coming to an end.)

"The room was dimly lit, with shadows creeping up the walls like tendrils of smoke." This imagery creates a sense of foreboding and could be used to describe a moment of tension or conflict.

"The scent of freshly baked bread filled the air, mingling with the sweet aroma of cinnamon and sugar." This imagery creates a sense of comfort and could be used to describe a moment of warmth or nostalgia.

"The waves crashed against the shore, sending up plumes of white foam and salt spray." This imagery creates a sense of movement and could be used to describe a particular location or environment.

"The air was heavy with the scent of pine needles and damp earth, reminding me of home." This imagery creates a sense of nostalgia and could be used to describe a particular time or place that holds emotional significance for the narrator.

By using imagery, you can create a sensory experience for your readers and help them connect more deeply with your experiences and emotions. However, it's important to use imagery in moderation and to ensure that your descriptions are relevant and appropriate to the narrative.

METAPHOR

Metaphors are powerful tools that can help readers understand complex ideas or emotions through comparisons to something more familiar. Here are some examples of using metaphors:

"Life is a journey." This common metaphor could be used to describe the ups and downs of life, as well as the idea of personal growth and self-discovery.

"The world was a blank canvas." This metaphor could be used to describe a moment of possibility or potential, such as starting a new project or a new adventure.

"Her heart was a shattered vase." This metaphor could be used to describe the pain of heartbreak or loss, and the feeling of being broken into pieces.

"The city was a living, breathing organism." This metaphor could be used to describe the energy and vitality of a bustling city, as well as the idea of a city being a complex system with its own rhythms and patterns.

"Memories are like bubbles, fragile and fleeting." This metaphor could be used to describe the ephemeral nature of memories, and how they can be easily lost or forgotten.

By using metaphors, you can create a stronger experience for the reader and help them connect with the emotions and experiences you are describing. However, it's important to use metaphors sparingly and thoughtfully, and to ensure that they are appropriate to the tone and style of your memoir.

FORESHADOWING

Hinting at events that will occur later in the story can create tension and keep readers engaged. Foreshadowing is a literary device used to give the reader a hint of what's to come in the story. Foreshadowing can be used to create anticipation and to draw attention to key themes or events. Here are some examples of foreshadowing:

> "Little did I know, this would be the last time I would see my grandmother alive." This foreshadows a future event, creates a sense of impending loss, and adds emotional weight to the scene.

> "I didn't realize it at the time, but this conversation would change the course of my life." This foreshadows a future turning point in the memoir, creating a sense of anticipation.

> "I had no idea what was coming, but looking back, I should have seen the signs." This foreshadows a future event that the reader is not yet aware of, creating suspense and intrigue.

> "As we drove away from the house, I couldn't shake the feeling that something bad was going to happen." This foreshadows a future conflict or crisis, creating a sense of unease and tension.

> "I thought I had everything figured out, but my biggest challenge was yet to come." This foreshadows a future struggle or obstacle, creating a sense of anticipation and setting up a dramatic arc for the memoir.

By using foreshadowing, you can create a sense of tension and anticipation that keeps readers invested in the story. However, too much foreshadowing can spoil the surprise and detract from the authenticity of your memoir, so it's important to use this device judiciously.

FLASHBACK

Using flashbacks can help provide context, convey background information, and deepen the reader's understanding of the story. Flashbacks can be a powerful tool, allowing the author to relive past experiences and offer readers insight into the events and emotions that shaped their life. However, using flashbacks effectively requires a delicate balance between providing enough context to make the past events understandable and avoiding overwhelming readers with too much information.

Here are some tips for using flashbacks in your memoir:

Make sure the flashback is necessary: Before including a flashback, ask yourself whether it's essential to the story you're telling. Does it provide valuable insight into your life or experiences? If not, consider leaving it out.

Use clear markers to signal the shift: Make it clear when you're shifting from the present to the past and back again. You can use phrases like "I remember" or "Back then" to signal the change.

Provide context: When you're writing a flashback, make sure to provide enough context to help the reader understand what's going on. You can do this by describing the setting, the people involved, and any relevant details.

Keep the focus on the present: Even when you're writing a flashback, it's important to keep the focus on the present moment of the story. Connect the past events to the present and show how they're relevant to the story you're telling.

Use sensory details: To bring the past to life, use sensory details to help the audience imagine the scene. Describe the sights, sounds, smells, and feelings of the past experience.

Avoid excessive use: While flashbacks can be a powerful tool, overusing them can be distracting and take away from the present story. Use them sparingly and only when necessary.

The goal of a memoir is to tell a compelling story that engages readers and offers insight into your life. Flashbacks can be a useful tool in achieving this goal, but they should be used thoughtfully and with care.

SYMBOLISM

Incorporating symbolic objects or images can add meaning and depth to the story. Here are some examples of using symbolism:

Tree: A tree can symbolize growth, resilience, and stability. In a memoir, a tree might represent a particular moment of growth or a personal transformation.

Water: Water can symbolize change, transformation, and renewal. In a memoir, water might represent a significant life event or a period of personal growth and transformation.

Mirror: A mirror can symbolize self-reflection and introspection. In a memoir, a mirror might represent a moment of self-discovery or a turning point in the narrator's story.

Butterfly: A butterfly can symbolize transformation, change, and rebirth. In a memoir, a butterfly might represent resilience and rebirth.

Key: A key can symbolize unlocking potential, gaining access, and overcoming obstacles. In a memoir, a key might represent a significant turning point, such as overcoming a personal obstacle or achieving a long-held goal.

Symbolism is a powerful tool that can add layers of meaning to your story. By using symbolism, you can create a deeper and more resonant reading experience for your audience. However, it's important to use symbolism sparingly and thoughtfully, and to ensure that your symbols are appropriate to the tone and style of your memoir.

IRONY

Irony is a literary device used to convey a meaning that is opposite to or different from its literal meaning. Irony can be used to create humor or tension, highlight contrasts, or add depth to a situation. Here are some categories of irony:

Situational Irony: This occurs when the outcome of a situation is different from what was expected. For example, a memoir about a fitness guru who develops a chronic illness could be considered situational irony. The irony lies in the fact that someone who promotes a healthy lifestyle is afflicted with a disease.

Dramatic Irony: This occurs when the reader knows something that the characters in the memoir do not. For example, a memoir about a young couple who are happily in love, but the reader knows that their relationship is going to end in a breakup, could be considered dramatic irony. The irony is in the contrast between the couple's happiness and the reader's knowledge of what's to come.

Verbal Irony: This occurs when the speaker says one thing but means the opposite. For example, a memoir about a person who hates being in the spotlight but ends up becoming a famous actor could be considered verbal irony. The irony is in the contrast between the person's desire for privacy and their eventual public success.

Cosmic Irony: This occurs when fate or destiny intervenes in a situation, often with a cruel or unexpected outcome. For example, a memoir about a person who dedicates their life to helping others but ends up needing help themselves could be considered cosmic irony. The irony lies in the fact that someone who spends their life being selfless is in a position of needing help.

Irony can be an effective literary tool, however, it's important to not overdo it, as too much irony can detract from the authenticity of your memoir.

HUMOR

Using humor in memoir writing can be a great way to engage readers and make your story more relatable and entertaining. Here are some examples of how humor can be used effectively in memoir:

Self-deprecating humor: Making fun of yourself and your own mistakes can be a great way to endear yourself to readers and make them feel more connected to you. For example, you could tell a funny story about a time when you made a foolish mistake or did something embarrassing.

Sarcasm: Using sarcasm can be an effective way to highlight the absurdities of life and make your story more entertaining. For example, you could write about a serious or dramatic event in a way that is deliberately humorous or ironic.

Observational humor: Paying attention to the small details of everyday life can be a great source of humor. You could write about the funny things you observe in your daily life or in the world around you.

Satire: Using satire to poke fun at societal norms or cultural expectations can be a powerful tool in memoir. You could write about a particular social or cultural issue that you find ridiculous or amusing, and use humor to make your point.

Wordplay: Playing with language and using puns or other forms of wordplay can be a fun way to inject humor into your writing. For example, you could use a pun in a title or subheading, or include a witty one-liner in your narrative.

Remember humor is subjective, so I'd suggest using it sparingly for strongest effect. Even if you're writing a humorous memoir, you want the "funny" to stand out.

Ultimately, the most effective literary devices will depend on the story being told and the author's unique voice and style. Experimenting with different techniques and finding which ones best serve the story and the author's voice are essential to crafting a successful memoir. Now you are familiar with some the most effective literary devices, which will help bring your memoir to life.

JOHN CHEEVER ON WRITING ABOUT PAIN

John Cheever always stressed to me the importance of writing about pain. In the 1970s, when I got to know Cheever, one of the most painful things in my life at the time was the fact that my father was an alcoholic. It was tearing our family apart. Cheever, of course, was famously an alcoholic himself, but had recently gotten clean for good when I met him. However, he would occasionally talk about his own struggles.

I remember one particular conversation when Cheever described his time teaching with the great short fiction writer Raymond Carver in Iowa during the early 1970s. He recounted how much they drank together, as if that was the sole focus of their days. It was during that conversation that I shared a little about my father, and I could tell Cheever picked up on the fact that my dad had a serious drinking problem.

In response, Cheever recommended I read his story called "Reunion," which he had written and had published in 1962. The story revolved around an awkward meeting between his son and his estranged father, and delved into the complexities of their relationship. I took his suggestion and read the story, and it had a profound impact on me.

I knew then that someday I would write about that pain. Cheever's advice and reading "Reunion" served as a catalyst for my own desire to express and explore my emotions through writing. I realized that painful experiences could be transformed into powerful narratives, allowing me to unpack the complexities of relationships, emotions, and personal growth.

However, I also understood that writing about such deeply personal and painful experiences would not be an easy task. It would require time, introspection, and a careful approach. It would be a therapeutic and cathartic process, helping me confront my emotions, gain insights into my family dynamics, and share my story with others who may have gone through similar challenges.

Writing about my father's alcoholism would not only be a means of self-expression, but also a way to raise awareness and provide support to individuals facing similar struggles. I believed that by sharing my experiences, I could help others find solace and understanding.

Today, as I reflect on those conversations with Cheever and the impact of "Reunion," I feel a growing sense of readiness. I am gradually preparing myself to write about that pain, to weave together the threads of my own story, and create something meaningful from the depths of my experiences.

Writing about pain is not an easy task, but I am determined to face it head-on. I know that through this process, I can find healing, growth, and the power to connect with others who have walked similar paths. Someday, I will share my story—not only for my own catharsis, but for others who may need it.

CHAPTER 15

Roman à Clef

A roman à clef is a type of novel that presents real-life people, events, or situations in a fictionalized form. The term "roman à clef" is French for "novel with a key," as the novel usually includes a key or guide to help readers identify the real-life people or events that inspired the fictionalized version. In a roman à clef, the author changes the names of the real-life people and often alters the events or situations to some degree, but the story is still recognizable as being based on true events. The purpose of a roman à clef is often to provide commentary or criticism on real-life situations or people while still maintaining a level of plausible deniability.

The use of a roman à clef can be a good idea for writing a memoir, as it allows the author to write about real-life experiences and people in a way that is less constrained by the factual details of the events. After all, crafting a roman à clef can help protect the privacy of the people involved in the memoir. By changing names and disguising identities, the author can write about personal experiences without exposing the real people involved. (But note, memoirs can change names for general privacy or legal reasons without being considered a roman à clef.)

Using a roman à clef can also provide the author with creative freedom to shape the story as they see fit. By fictionalizing some details or events, the author can create a more compelling narrative that better captures the essence of their experiences. A roman à clef can also add an element of intrigue to the memoir. By presenting real events and people in a fictionalized form, the reader is left to wonder what is fact and what is fiction, which can make for a more enjoyable read. A roman à clef allows the author to reflect on and interpret their experiences in a way that goes beyond the mere retelling of events. By adding a layer of interpretation and analysis to the story, the memoir can become more meaningful for readers.

Of course, it's important for the author to be transparent about their use of a roman à clef and to make it clear to readers what is fact and what is fiction. But when used appropriately, a roman à clef can be a powerful tool for writing creative nonfiction that is both personal and universal in its appeal. But of course, it's not a traditional "memoir" because the memoir form is purely nonfiction.

There have been many examples of roman à clef throughout literary history. Here are a few notable ones:

The Sun Also Rises by Ernest Hemingway: This novel is widely believed to be a roman à clef based on Hemingway's own experiences as an expatriate in Paris in the 1920s. The characters are based on real people, including Hemingway himself, and the events of the story are based on actual events that Hemingway witnessed.

Animal Farm by George Orwell: Although this book is a fable, it is an example of a roman à clef in that it uses animals to represent real-life people and events. The book is a satirical commentary on the Russian Revolution and Stalinist Russia, with the character of Napoleon representing Stalin.

To Kill a Mockingbird by Harper Lee: This classic is believed to be based on Lee's own experiences growing up in Alabama in the 1930s. The character of Atticus Finch is considered to be inspired by Lee's own father, who was a lawyer and defended African American clients.

The Bell Jar by Sylvia Plath: This novel is a semi-autobiographical work that is believed to be based on Plath's own experiences as a young woman struggling with mental illness. The character of Esther Greenwood is believed to be a fictionalized version of Plath herself.

Some find the method of using a roman à clef to be incredibly helpful for several reasons. Speaking from personal experience, I believe this approach can be advantageous for multiple reasons.

First and foremost, employing a roman à clef allows you to protect the privacy and identities of the real people in your life. As much as you may want to share personal experiences and stories, it's good to also respect the boundaries and wishes of those involved. By fictionalizing characters and events, you can maintain a level of privacy and confidentiality, offering a sense of security to both yourself and the individuals who may be part of your story.

Beyond privacy concerns, using a roman à clef opens up a world of creative possibilities. Writing a memoir is about more than just recounting facts and events—it's about capturing the essence of your experiences and emotions. By incorporating fictional elements, you can explore different perspectives, add depth to characters, and infuse your story with symbolism and metaphor.

The roman à clef technique enables you to delve into the subjective nature of memory and perception. As a memoirist, you understand that your recollection of events might not align precisely with objective reality. By embracing the fictionalization of characters and situations, you can emphasize your own perspective, emotions, and growth throughout your memoir. It allows you to paint a more authentic picture of your experiences, capturing the essence of your personal truth.

Another advantage of the roman à clef method is the intriguing interplay between fact and fiction. Blurring the lines between reality and imagination can add an extra layer of complexity and engagement to your memoir. It prompts readers to question the boundaries of truth, memory, and storytelling, inviting them to become active participants in the narrative. This dynamic can spark conversations and reflections, creating a deeper connection between you and your readers.

Finally, using a roman à clef can provide a sense of protection from potential legal or ethical concerns. Not everyone in your life may be comfortable with their stories being shared openly, and you may want to respect their wishes. By fictionalizing elements of your memoir, you can reduce the risk of conflicts or repercussions while still staying true to the essence of your experiences.

The method of writing your story using a roman à clef has proven to be incredibly helpful for many. It allows one to protect privacy, unleash creativity, explore subjectivity, engage readers in the interplay between fact and fiction, and ensure ethical considerations are met. Ultimately, it empowers one to share their story authentically while respecting the boundaries and complexities of personal relationships.

Is using a roman à clef right for you? That's up to you to decide.

YOUR "LITERARY FINGERPRINT"

When it comes to writing a memoir, one must always consider the importance of embracing their own uniqueness. Each individual possesses what can be referred to as a "literary fingerprint"—a distinct voice and perspective that sets them apart from anyone else. It is crucial to never underestimate the significance of your own voice, which is special and unique in its own way.

A memoir is a personal account of one's own experiences, emotions, and reflections. It delves into the depths of your life, capturing significant moments, challenges, triumphs, and personal growth. It is through your distinct voice that these stories come alive, resonating with readers in a way that only you can achieve.

Your experiences and thoughts are unlike anyone else's. You have lived a life filled with a multitude of moments—both big and small—that have shaped you into the person you are today. Your perspective is influenced by your background, values, and beliefs, which are entirely unique to you. Therefore, when writing your memoir, it is essential to embrace this individuality and let it shine through your words.

Sometimes, writers doubt the significance of their own voice. They may compare themselves to others, or believe that their experiences are not extraordinary enough to captivate readers. However, it is precisely these doubts that need to be challenged. The beauty of a memoir lies in its relatability. Readers are drawn to genuine stories that reflect the human condition and offer insights into the shared experiences of life. What may seem ordinary to you can resonate deeply with someone who has gone through similar situations or emotions.

Remember that your voice adds a layer of authenticity to your memoir. It is a reflection of who you are as a person, and it carries the power to connect with others on a meaningful level. By embracing your unique perspective, you give readers the opportunity to see the world through your eyes, to empathize with your struggles, and to celebrate your triumphs.

While it can be inspiring to learn from other writers and explore different styles and techniques, it is crucial to avoid imitating or trying to be someone else when writing your memoir. Your voice is an asset that sets you apart. Embrace it, nurture it, and let it guide your storytelling.

Honor your unique experiences, emotions, and thoughts. Embrace the fact that your literary fingerprint is one-of-a-kind. Your voice is special, and it will connect with readers who appreciate and value what only you can provide. Celebrate your uniqueness, and trust that your memoir has the power to touch hearts, inspire minds, and leave a lasting mark.

CHAPTER 16

So Now What?

Okay, so those are most of the basics. With these fundamental tools in your possession, you now find yourself preparing to embark on a voyage that is as diverse and multifaceted as each individual who undertakes it. In my opinion, memoir writing is not a complex enigma or an elusive code to crack. It is not a privilege reserved for a select few who possess an innate genius or a mastery of language. No, it is a craft that can be approached with simplicity and directness. It is a process that demands honesty, vulnerability, and a deep-rooted desire to share one's truth with the world.

Yet, even as we equip ourselves with the knowledge and techniques necessary to navigate the literary waters, it is essential to acknowledge a fundamental truth: every writer, every *individual*, possesses a unique path. As we embark on a metaphorical road trip cross country—each in our separate cars—we may share the same destination, but the roads we traverse, the stops we make, and the experiences we encounter along the way will be distinct and diverse. It is this diversity of perspective that shapes the stories we have to tell, infusing them with richness, nuance, and an unparalleled sense of individuality.

In memoir writing, we are granted the freedom to explore the vast and varied landscapes of our lives. We are encouraged to navigate the winding roads of memory, to contemplate the peaks and valleys of our experiences, and to select the moments that resonate most deeply within our hearts. It is through these deliberate choices that we begin to mold and shape our narratives, weaving together the tapestry of our lives with the threads of introspection, reflection, and the unyielding pursuit of truth.

Writing a memoir is, without a doubt, a journey—a transformative odyssey, a pilgrimage to the depths of our emotions, and a quest to capture the essence of our lives on the page. As with any journey, once we set our sights on a destination, it becomes our responsibility—our privilege—to chart our own course. We become the captains of our memoir ships, navigating the tides of our past, present, and future with unwavering determination and an insatiable thirst for self-expression.

And so, I implore you to embrace the uniqueness of your voice, your perspective, and your path. Celebrate the beauty of your own story, for it is a story that only *you* can tell—a narrative that encapsulates the triumphs, the trials, the joys, and the sorrows that have shaped you into the remarkable individual you are today. Allow yourself the freedom to experiment, to take risks, and to dive deep into the recesses of your memory, unearthing the treasures that lie dormant within.

The destination is undeniably significant. However, it is the trip itself—the process of introspection, self-discovery, and storytelling—that unfurls the magic hidden within our experiences. It is in the act of weaving together our memories.

For me, the conclusion of a workshop or class often brings a sense of loss—an absence of weekly expectations and assignments that have propelled us forward. However, this is precisely the moment when we must rise above the temptation to let our pens grow idle.

In the absence of a structured environment, writers' groups become invaluable. They provide a supportive community that helps sustain the motivation and discipline required to keep writing. Engaging with fellow writers, sharing our work, and receiving feedback can be an invigorating experience. These groups remind us that we are not alone and that our stories deserve to be heard.

In recognition of the challenges that lie ahead, I have included numerous prompts in this book. They are not gentle reminders, but powerful nudges—urging you to continue writing on a daily basis. Writing is more than a creative outlet; it is a cathartic and transformative exercise. It allows us to make sense of our lives, to weave meaning into our experiences, and find solace or purpose in our narratives.

Regardless of whether your ultimate goal is to have your memoir published, the act of writing itself is a healthy exercise. It is a way to process emotions, confront demons, and celebrate triumphs. It enables us to distill our thoughts, gain clarity, and find a deeper understanding of ourselves. Writing is an act of self-care, an expression of our unique voice, and a testament to our existence.

For those of you who do aspire to see your memoirs in print, I must emphasize the importance of committing to a disciplined writing schedule. It is no secret that the path to publication is arduous and filled with challenges. It demands dedication, perseverance, and unwavering commitment. But it is precisely this dedication—the willingness to show up, day after day, and put pen to paper—that will set you apart.

Writing is not meant to be easy; however, it is in the struggle and effort that we find the most substantial rewards. Through the discipline of writing, we refine our skills, hone our craft, and give life to our stories. It is in these moments of persistence that we find our true potential as writers, as storytellers, and as individuals. Let us remember that writing is not confined to the walls of a classroom or the pages of a book. It is a lifelong pursuit—an ongoing conversation with ourselves and the world around us.

I encourage you to create a writing routine that suits your life. Carve out time each day to honor your craft and embrace the challenges that lie ahead. Seek out writers' groups, attend workshops, and never shy away from seeking feedback and con-structive criticism. Remember that the power of your story lies in your willingness to share it with others. Whether you choose to pursue publication or simply write for personal fulfillment, your words have the potential to touch lives, inspire change, and create connections.

Embrace the uncertainty that comes with the writing pro-cess. Allow yourself to explore new ideas, experiment with dif-ferent styles, and take risks with your storytelling. Embrace the joy of discovery and the beauty of revision. Know that every word you write, every sentence you craft, brings you closer to becoming the writer you aspire to be.

Above all, be kind to yourself. Writing can be a demanding endeavor. There will be moments of self-doubt, creative blocks, and the nagging voice of your inner critic. But remember that writing is a journey, and every step forward—no matter how small—is still an achievement. Celebrate your progress, acknowledge your growth, and find solace in the act of creation itself.

Remember that what I have shared in this book is just the beginning. The true value lies in what you do with the knowledge and skills you have gained. Carry the momentum forward, continue to write, and nurture your writer's soul. Your story matters, and the world is waiting to hear it.

WORKING WITH TYRUS

When I started working with former pro wrestler and political news commentator Tyrus on his memoir, I was struck by the intensity and drama of his tortured childhood. The scars ran deep—were etched into his soul—but he was reticent to write about it. He believed it was too personal. His childhood was a dark secret he had never really confronted before.

I believed delving into his upbringing was crucial to laying the foundation for his story. It was the key to unlocking the depths of his experiences and understanding the person he had become. We went back and forth on the topic, standing at the crossroads of our collaboration, unsure of which path to take. The divide between us grew, friendly but firm. Days passed, and I couldn't shake the weight of our differences. Then, my phone rang one evening. It was Tyrus. His voice sounded different, resolute. He said, "You've written a lot of books, and this is my first. I'm going to trust you. I think I'm ready to tackle this." His words struck a chord with me. I knew the significance of what he was about to do. It was a turning point, a moment of bravery. Together, we took a leap of faith.

Tyrus poured his heart onto the pages, revisiting painful memories and confronting demons that had haunted him for so long. He bared his soul, unearthing the truth that had been buried within. It wasn't easy. It was raw, unsettling, and at times, agonizing. But it was necessary.

Two weeks before the book was set to be released, Tyrus called me. His voice was tinged with uncertainty. He asked if I thought the entire project could be pulled from production. I was taken aback by his sudden change of heart. "No way," I responded firmly. "The book has been printed. It's probably on its way to bookstores as we speak."

Tyrus explained his second thoughts. Nagging doubts had crept in as the realization sank in that his most intimate story would soon be in the hands of readers worldwide. I reassured him, understanding his apprehension all too well. That last moment before the world becomes privy to your story can be a whirlwind of emotions—excitement and fear intertwined.

"It's normal to feel this way," I told him. "Releasing something so personal to the world is a monumental step, and it's natural to be both excited and scared. Your truth on the page is what makes your story so powerful."

I empathized with Tyrus, assuring him that everything would be okay. His feelings were valid, and it was crucial to acknowledge the significance of this moment. But we couldn't reverse the release of the book. I reminded him that he had made the right decision and that his bravery in sharing his truth was admirable.

"Remember," I said, "when you release your story to the world, a little bit of anxiety on the cusp of release is completely understandable. In fact, it's healthy. It means you've poured your heart into something that matters deeply to you."

We talked for a while, discussing the rollercoaster of emotions that often accompanies such a significant milestone. I shared stories of other authors who had experienced similar apprehensions before their books were released and how they eventually found solace in the knowledge that their stories could impact others.

By the end of our conversation, Tyrus seemed more at ease. He understood that his vulnerability was what would connect readers to his story; his life could inspire and touch lives. The book would be released as planned, and while the anticipation remained, he embraced the knowledge that he had taken a courageous step in sharing his truth.

In the end, the release of Tyrus's memoir was met with overwhelming support and appreciation from readers. His story touched hearts, sparked conversations, and offered solace to those who had experienced similar struggles. It also became a huge success, not solely because of his eloquent prose or captivating storytelling, but because he had confronted something powerful and painful right at the beginning. That moment set the tone for what was to follow—an unflinching exploration of truth, resilience, and the human spirit.

Reflecting on our writing experience, I realized the lesson we had learned together. Even though it may seem scary and uncomfortable, confronting your truth is vital. It is the path to healing, growth, and authenticity. Tyrus's memoir stands as a testament to that truth—a beacon for others to find the courage to face their own stories, no matter how difficult they may be.

CHAPTER 17

The Business of Writing

Whether you dream of securing a traditional publishing deal or exploring self-publishing options, understanding the intricacies of the business side of writing is essential. My hope is that this chapter provides you with valuable insights, guidance, and inspiration, empowering you to make informed choices and begin a fruitful start toward sharing your memoir with the world. Writing a memoir is an art, but successfully selling it is a business. So let's delve into the business of writing and discover the possibilities that await you.

It's only natural to wonder about the practical aspects of turning your passion into a successful venture. Many aspiring authors dream of sharing their personal stories with the world, and some of them are eager to explore selling their work. Writing a memoir is a deeply personal endeavor, but understanding the business aspects of the publishing industry can significantly impact your chances of success. With the right knowledge and approach, you can navigate the complex landscape of selling your story and ensure that your voice reaches the widest possible audience.

In this chapter, I will explore the key components involved in selling your work—from writing proposals to insights into the roles, responsibilities, and functions of literary agents and publishers. I will discuss the benefits of securing an agent, the process of finding representation, and the crucial role these professionals play in negotiating contracts and protecting your interests. I will also cover the responsibilities of publishers, who act as the bridge between your manuscript and the readership you aspire to reach. Understanding their role in editing, marketing, and distribution will help you make informed decisions as you navigate the publishing landscape.

WHY GET AN AGENT?

When you sell your memoir, your literary agent plays an important role in representing your interests and negotiating the terms of your publishing contract. Here are some of the key tasks your literary agent may do for you when you sell your memoir:

1. **Submit your book to publishers**: Your literary agent will submit your manuscript to publishing houses that are a good fit for your work, leveraging their industry contacts and knowledge of the publishing landscape to get your book in front of the right people.

2. **Negotiate your contract**: Your literary agent will negotiate the terms of your publishing contract on your behalf, ensuring that you are paid fairly and that your interests are protected. They will advocate for you on issues such as advance payments, royalty rates, and rights to your work.

3. **Provide editorial feedback**: Before submitting your manuscript to publishers, your literary agent may pro-

vide feedback and guidance on your writing, helping you to refine your work and make it more marketable.

4. **Offer industry insight**: Your literary agent will keep you informed about industry trends, including what is selling well in the market and what publishers are looking for in a memoir. This can help you position your work in the best possible way and increase your chances of getting published.

5. **Build your brand**: Your literary agent may work with you to build your brand as an author, helping you to develop your author platform, secure speaking engagements, and build your online presence.

Your literary agent is your advocate and partner throughout the publishing process. They will work tirelessly to ensure that you get the best possible deal and that your memoir reaches the widest possible audience.

Attaining a literary agent for your memoir can be a challenging process, but there are a few steps you can take to increase your chances of success.

HOW TO GET AN AGENT

1. **Write a strong query letter**: Your query letter is the first impression an agent will have of your memoir, so it's important to make it as compelling and polished as possible. Your letter should include a brief summary of your book, an explanation of why you are the best person to write it, and any relevant writing credentials or platforms you have.

2. **Research literary agents who represent memoirs**: Look for agents who have a track record of representing memoirs in your genre and style. You can find agents through online directories—such as AgentQuery. com or Publishers Marketplace—or by researching books similar to yours and finding out who represents those authors.

3. **Follow submission guidelines carefully**: Each literary agent will have specific submission guidelines, so be sure to read them carefully and follow them to the letter. Failure to do so may result in your query being rejected without being read.

4. **Network and attend writing conferences**: Attending writing conferences and networking with other writers and publishing professionals can be a great way to make connections and learn about agents who may be a good fit for your memoir.

5. **Be patient and persistent**: Finding a literary agent can be a slow and frustrating process, so it's important to be patient and persistent. Keep submitting to agents who are a good fit for your memoir, and be open to feedback and revision suggestions.

The key to acquiring a literary agent for your memoir is to have a strong and compelling story, and to be persistent and professional in your submission process.

Rejection is a common part of the writing and publishing process, and can be especially difficult when it comes to submitting your memoir. Here are some tips for dealing with rejection:

1. **Don't take it personally**: Remember that rejection is not a reflection of your worth as a writer or as a person. Literary agents and publishers receive many submissions and have to make tough decisions about which ones to accept. Rejection doesn't mean your writing isn't good or that your story isn't important.
2. **Keep things in perspective**: While it's easy to focus on the rejections, it's important to remember that each rejection is one person's opinion. Just because one agent or publisher didn't connect with your memoir doesn't mean that others won't. Keep submitting and stay focused on your goal.
3. **Take time to process your emotions**: It's natural to feel disappointed, frustrated, or even angry when you receive a rejection. Take some time to acknowledge and process these emotions, but try not to dwell on them for too long.
4. **Keep writing and revising**: Use rejection as an opportunity to improve your writing and your memoir. Take any feedback you receive seriously, and use it to revise and improve your work. Keep writing new material and honing your craft.
5. **Seek support**: Writing can be a solitary pursuit, but it's important to seek support from others when you're dealing with rejection. Join a writing group, seek out a writing coach or mentor, or connect with other writers online. Having a supportive community can help you stay motivated and keep you moving forward.

Rejection is a natural part of the writing and publishing process. By staying focused on your goals, improving your craft, and seeking support, you can navigate rejection and continue to move closer to your goal of publishing your memoir.

WHAT TO ASK AGENTS

If you are a memoir author looking for representation by an agent, here are some questions you may want to ask before signing a contract:

What is your experience with memoirs?

You should ask about the agent's experience with memoirs to ensure that they understand the market and the unique challenges of the genre.

What is your approach to representing authors?

You should inquire about the agent's process and philosophy of working with authors to ensure that their approach aligns with your goals and expectations.

What publishers do you have relationships with?

You should ask about the agent's connections with publishers to get an idea of their ability to place your memoir with a reputable publisher.

What is your strategy for submitting my memoir to publishers?

You should ask about the agent's submission strategy, including how many publishers they plan to submit to and how they plan to pitch your memoir to these publishers.

What is your track record for representing authors in the memoir genre?

You should ask about the agent's history with securing publishing deals for memoir authors and what kind of advance they typically secure for their clients.

What are your commission rates and contract terms?

You should ask about the agent's commission rates and contract terms to ensure that they are fair and reasonable.

How do you handle conflicts of interest?

You should inquire about how the agent handles potential conflicts of interest and whether they have any existing relationships with publishers that may pose a conflict of interest.

By asking these questions, you can get a better understanding of the agent's experience, strategy, and approach to representing memoir authors. It's important to make an informed decision about who to work with.

Must you have an agent? No. In today's publishing landscape, aspiring memoirists have more options than ever when it comes to getting their work published. While literary agents can be immensely helpful in navigating the publishing industry, it is not always necessary to have one to sell your memoir. There are numerous small to midsize publishers who are open to direct submissions from authors, which is a viable alternative for those seeking to bypass the traditional agent route.

The process of submitting your memoir directly to publishers typically involves the following steps:

1. **Research**: Begin by researching publishers who special-
    ize in memoir or have a track record of publishing sim-
    ilar works. Look for publishers whose values, interests,
    and target audience align with your own memoir. Make
    sure to thoroughly review their submission guidelines,
    which can usually be found on their websites.

2. **Preparing your manuscript**: Before submitting, ensure
    that your memoir is complete, edited, and polished.
    It's important to present a professional and well-crafted
    manuscript to publishers. Consider seeking feedback
    from beta readers or a professional editor to improve the
    overall quality and structure of your work.

3. **Writing a compelling query letter**: A query letter serves
    as your introduction to the publisher and should entice
    them to request your manuscript. It should be concise
    and highlight the unique aspects of your memoir. Your
    letter should include a brief synopsis, information about
    your background as an author, and why you believe your
    memoir would resonate with readers.

4. **Crafting a professional book proposal**: Book propos-
    als are essential for nonfiction works, and of course that
    includes memoir submissions. A book proposal typi-
    cally includes an overview of your memoir, an analy-
    sis of the target market and competition, a summary
    of your author platform, and a sample chapter or two.
    A book proposal helps publishers assess the commercial
    viability of your memoir.

5. **Submitting your materials**: Follow each publisher's
    submission guidelines carefully. Some may prefer email
    submissions, while others may require physical copies.

Include your query letter, book proposal (if applicable), and any other materials requested by the publisher.

6. **Waiting for a response**: The waiting period can vary significantly from publisher to publisher. It's important to be patient and understand that the review process takes time. Some publishers may respond within a few weeks, while others may take several months. In the meantime, you can continue working on your writing or explore other publishing avenues. It's ok to submit to multiple publishers at once, but do it sparingly. Target publishers that truly seem like a good fit for your story.

7. **Evaluating offers**: If a publisher expresses interest in your memoir, they may request additional materials or invite you to discuss the possibility of publication. It is important to carefully review any offers you receive, including the terms of the contract, royalty rates, marketing support, and rights they are seeking.

8. **Making a decision**: Once you've received offers, evaluate each publisher's reputation, track record, and the overall fit of the publisher with your goals and vision for your memoir. Consider seeking advice from other authors or industry professionals if needed. Ultimately, choose the publisher that aligns best with your aspirations and offers the most advantageous terms.

While direct submissions to publishers can be a viable option, it's still important to research and approach reputable publishers who have a history of successfully publishing and promoting memoirs. Working with a literary agent can provide valuable industry insights, negotiation expertise, and access to larger publishing houses. The decision to pursue direct submissions or seek representation ultimately depends on your individual preferences and goals as an author.

THE PROPOSAL

A memoir proposal is a document that outlines your memoir project and pitches it to literary agents or publishers. Here are some tips on how to write a strong memoir proposal:

1. **Start with a compelling hook**: Begin your proposal with a compelling opening that draws the agent or publisher in and makes them want to learn more about your story.

2. **Provide a summary of your memoir**: Give a brief summary of your memoir, including the central themes, plot, and key characters.

3. **Describe your target audience**: Explain who your book is intended for and why you think it will appeal to this audience.

4. **Outline your platform**: Describe your platform as a writer, including any previous publications or writing experience, as well as your social media presence.

5. **Discuss your marketing plan**: Explain how you plan to market your book and reach your target audience, including any book tour plans or media appearances.

6. **Include a sample chapter**: Include a polished sample chapter from your memoir to give the reader a sense of your writing style and the tone of your book.

7. **Provide a detailed author bio**: Include a thorough-but-concise author bio that highlights your cre-

dentials and any relevant experience that makes you uniquely qualified to tell your story.

Remember that a memoir proposal should be professional and concise. It should showcase your writing skills and demonstrate that you have a unique and compelling story to tell.

SELF-PUBLISHING

Self-publishing can be a viable option for authors who want to bring their memoir to readers without going through traditional publishing routes. It allows you to maintain creative control over your work and take charge of the entire publishing process. Self-publishing a memoir has both pros and cons, which I've outlined below.

Pros

Control: One of the biggest advantages of self-publishing is that the author has complete control over the content, cover design, marketing, and distribution of their book. This allows the author to retain creative control and make decisions about how their work is presented to the public.

Speed: Self-publishing can often be a faster process than traditional publishing, as the author does not have to go through the lengthy submission and approval process of a traditional publishing house.

Profit: In self-publishing, authors typically retain a higher percentage of the profits compared to traditional publishing. While traditional publishers may offer authors royalties in the range of 10–25 percent of the book's net profits, self-published authors often retain 60–70 percent of the retail price of each book sold through platforms like Amazon's Kindle Direct Publishing (KDP). Many self-published authors do not break even due to the costs involved, especially if they do not effectively market their work. However, some self-published authors are able to turn a profit, particularly if they have a strong marketing strategy, a dedicated readership, and produce high-quality, in-demand content. Success in self-publishing often depends on the author's ability to effectively navigate the complexities of the publishing industry, engage with their audience, and produce compelling, marketable work.

Flexibility: Self-publishing allows the author to experiment with different formats and publishing strategies, such as offering the book in multiple formats or distributing it through various online platforms.

Cons

Quality: Self-publishing can result in lower-quality books, as the author may not have access to professional editing, design, and printing services that are typically provided by a traditional publishing house.

Marketing: Self-publishing requires the author to take sole responsibility of marketing, which can be time-consuming and challenging for those without experience in book promotion.

Credibility: Self-published books may be perceived as less credible or less prestigious than traditionally published books, which can make it more difficult for the author to gain recognition or acceptance within the literary community.

Cost: Self-publishing can be expensive, as the author must cover the cost of editing, design, printing, and marketing.

Self-publishing a memoir can offer greater control, speed, profit, and flexibility. But it can also result in lower quality products, more marketing responsibilities, less credibility, and greater expense. It is important for authors to weigh the pros and cons and make an informed decision about which publishing route is best for their specific needs and goals.

HOW AUTHORS TRADITIONALLY GET PAID

Authors are typically paid two ways when they sell a book: through an advance and through royalties.

Advance: When a book publisher buys the rights to publish an author's book, they usually pay the author an advance against future royalties. This is an upfront payment that is intended to cover the author's living expenses while they write the book, as well as to provide some income for the author while the book is being edited and prepared for publication. The size of the advance will depend on a number of factors, including the author's reputation, the book's potential market, and the publisher's budget. Advances for first-time authors can range from a few thousand dollars to tens of thousands of dollars, while advances for established bestselling authors can reach into the millions.

It's important to note that not all authors receive an advance, especially first-time authors or authors still establishing their reputation. In these cases, authors may receive only royalties for their book sales. In addition, authors may receive other forms of compensation for their work—such as speaking fees, book signings, and other promotional events.

Royalties: Once the book is published and sold, the author will earn royalties on each copy sold. Royalties are typically a percentage of the book's retail price, ranging from 5–15 percent for print books and 20–25 percent (even up to 70 percent) for eBooks. The royalty rate is negotiated between the author and the publisher as part of the book contract. The amount of royalties earned by an author can vary widely depending on the book's sales, the price point, and the royalty rate. For example, an author may only earn a few cents per book sold, while in other cases, they may earn several dollars.

Publishers typically calculate and pay royalties on a regular basis, usually twice a year or quarterly. The amount of royalties earned by an author is usually based on the number of copies of the book sold during that period. The publisher will also deduct any expenses related to the production and marketing of the book before calculating the author's royalties. There are some variations in how authors are paid by publishers, depending on the type of book and the publisher's policies. For example, some publishers may offer a "royalty advance" in which the author receives a lump sum payment upfront that is later deducted from their future royalties. Additionally, some publishers may offer different royalty rates for different formats of the book, such as eBooks, audiobooks, or foreign language editions.

Generally, the payment structure for authors can be complex, and it's important for authors to carefully review and negotiate their contracts with publishers to ensure that they are being fairly compensated for their work. (I will add that if you are ghostwriting a project with someone, oftentimes that results in a flat fee being paid to you without any sort of royalty sharing. That's called a "buyout" and it's quite common in the ghostwriting business.)

WORKING WITH AN EDITOR

Working with an editor on your memoir can be an enriching and empowering experience. It can help you refine your story, improve your writing, and bring your vision for your book to life. Here are a few things you can expect when collaborating with an editor on your memoir, either through a publisher or your own freelancer:

Objective feedback: An editor can provide objective feedback on your work, offering a fresh perspective that can help you see your writing in a new light. They can identify areas where your writing needs improvement, point out inconsistencies in your story, and help you refine your voice and style.

Support and guidance: A good editor will be your advocate and guide, helping you navigate the sometimes overwhelming process of writing a memoir. They can provide resources and tools to improve your writing, and offer support and encouragement throughout the process.

Collaboration: While an editor will provide feedback and guidance, they are also there to collaborate with you on your memoir. They will work with you to understand your vision for the book and help you craft a narrative that is compelling and true to your experience.

Revisions and edits: Expect to receive feedback on your work and to go through a process of revisions and edits. This is a normal part of the editing process and can be incredibly valuable in helping you refine your story and improve your writing.

Respect for your story: A good editor understands that your memoir is deeply personal and meaningful to you. They will treat your story with respect and work with you to ensure that your voice and perspective are honored throughout the editing process. Remember to vet editors just as you would an agent or a publisher, as they are just as important to your project.

WHAT TO ASK A PUBLISHER

If you have the opportunity to work with a publisher, these are some of the questions I would ask them:

What is your publishing process and timeline?

It's essential to understand the steps the publisher takes to produce and distribute your memoir, including editing, cover design, typesetting, printing, and distribution. You will also need to know how long each step takes so you can plan accordingly.

What marketing and promotion strategies do you have in place?

You should inquire about how the publisher plans to market and promote your memoir to potential readers. You can also discuss your marketing efforts and come up with a plan that works for you and your publisher.

What is your approach to editing and revising the manuscript?

It's important to ask how much editorial control you have and what changes the publisher expects you to make to the manuscript. It's also essential to understand how many rounds of editing the publisher will perform and whether they will use a professional editor.

What are the royalty rates and what is the payment schedule?

It's crucial to understand the financial aspect of the publishing contract. You should ask about the percentage of royalties you'll receive and when you'll receive payments.

Will you receive physical copies of the book?

You should ask about how many copies of the book you'll receive and whether you'll have to pay for them.

What is the publisher's policy on copyright and intellectual property?

You should ask about who holds the rights to your memoir and whether the publisher will obtain permissions for any copyrighted materials used in the book.

What is the publisher's distribution reach?

You should inquire about where the publisher distributes the book and how it will be made available to readers. You can also ask about international distribution, if applicable.

WHEN IS A BOOK CONSIDERED "FINANCIALLY SUCCESSFUL"?

The world of publishing can be a fickle one, and it's often difficult to determine what constitutes financial success for a book. While there is no one-size-fits-all answer to this question, there are several factors that can help determine whether a book is financially successful or not.

One of the primary factors that contributes to financial success for a book is the number of copies sold. As a general rule of thumb, a book that sells fewer than 5,000 copies is considered a commercial failure, while a book that sells over 100,000 copies is considered a commercial success. However, these figures can vary widely depending on the author's genre, the book's price point, and the publisher's expectations.

For example, a niche book that targets a specific audience may not need to sell as many copies to be considered financially successful, as long as the publisher is able to keep production and marketing costs low. Similarly, a high-priced art book or cookbook may not need to sell as many copies to be considered successful, as each sale generates a higher profit margin.

Another factor that can contribute to financial success for a book is its adaptation into film or television. If a book is adapted into a successful movie or TV show, it can generate significant additional income for the author. However, it's worth noting that the process of adapting a book into a movie or TV show can be complex, and not all books are suitable for adaptation.

Finally, financial success can also be influenced by speaking engagements, merchandise sales, and other related income streams. For example, a bestselling author may be able to charge high fees for speaking engagements and may also sell merchandise related to their book (such as t-shirts, mugs, or other items).

Ultimately, financial success as an author depends on a combination of factors, and there is no single formula for achieving it. However, by focusing on writing quality books that resonate with readers, building a loyal fan base, and diversifying income streams, authors can increase their chances of achieving financial success in the publishing industry.

BUILDING YOUR PLATFORM

As mentioned earlier in this chapter, creating a platform for yourself can add credibility to your writing when approaching agents and publishers. Platforms such as Medium and Substack, among several others, provide simple ways for you to build an audience by sharing your stories. These platforms offer various benefits that can help you gain followers and showcase your writing prowess, which agents and publishers often value.

Medium and Substack are popular platforms where writers can self-publish their work and attract a following. By consistently sharing your stories and engaging with the platform's community, you can gradually build a dedicated audience who appreciate your writing style and storytelling abilities. Having a sizable following demonstrates that your work connects with readers and can make an impression on agents and publishers.

These platforms provide tools and features that allow you to target specific audiences based on interests, genres, or topics. You can utilize tags, categories, or keywords to ensure your work reaches the audience most likely to be interested in your memoir. This targeted approach helps you connect with the right audience and potentially attract agents and publishers who specialize in your genre or subject matter.

As you post on platforms like Medium and Substack, you have the opportunity to accumulate social proof in the form of likes, comments, and shares. Positive engagement can validate your writing skills and storytelling ability. Agents and publishers often take note of the level of reader engagement and social proof your work receives, as it demonstrates that your writing has the potential to resonate with a wider audience.

Building a platform allows you to showcase your writing portfolio and provide writing samples to interested agents and publishers. You can curate a collection of your best stories or excerpts from your memoir, making it easier for industry professionals to assess your writing style and the quality of your work. This can create a positive impression and increase your chances of getting noticed by agents or publishers.

Creating a platform helps you establish and strengthen your author brand. By consistently sharing your stories with readers and cultivating a unique writing voice, you can develop a recognizable brand identity. This branding can make you stand out among other writers and demonstrate to agents and publishers that you have the potential to build a loyal readership.

Remember that building a platform and gaining credibility through platforms like Medium and Substack takes time, effort, and consistent engagement. It's essential to create high-quality content, interact with your audience, and actively promote your work through various channels. By doing so, you can enhance your chances of attracting the attention of agents and publishers who value a strong platform and engaged readership.

As well, budding authors can utilize social media platforms like YouTube, Instagram, Facebook, X (formerly Twitter), TikTok, etc., to engage with potential readers by sharing behind-the-scenes insights, writing tips, book excerpts, and personal stories. By consistently posting valuable and engaging content, authors can attract followers who are interested in their work. Publishers value authors with a strong social media presence as it demonstrates their ability to connect with an audience and build a platform for promoting their books effectively, ultimately contributing to a successful marketing campaign.

MARKETING

Marketing a memoir can be challenging, but there are several effective strategies that can help you reach your target audience and generate interest in your book. Here are some of the best ways to market your memoir:

Seek reviews and endorsements: Reach out to book bloggers, book clubs, and other literary influencers to request reviews and endorsements for your memoir. Positive reviews and endorsements can help generate buzz and interest in your book.

Offer giveaways and promotions: Consider offering giveaways, discounts, or other promotions to entice potential readers to purchase your book. You could offer a free chapter or a signed copy of your book to those who sign up for your newsletter or follow you on social media.

Attend book festivals and events: Book festivals and events can be a great way to connect with people and promote your memoir. Look for local book festivals and author events in your area, and consider participating in author panels or readings to showcase your book.

Leverage online advertising: Consider using online advertising platforms—such as Google Ads, Facebook Ads, or Amazon Ads—to target readers who are interested in memoirs. This can be an effective way to reach a wider audience and generate more book sales.

Network with other authors and literary professionals: Attend literary events and conferences to connect with other authors and literary professionals, and consider joining writing groups or associations to build your network and promote your memoir.

Marketing your memoir is an ongoing process, and it may take time and effort to build a readership and generate interest in your book. By using a combination of these strategies and staying engaged with your audience, you can successfully promote your memoir and reach a wider audience.

WORKING WITH DONA SPEIR

When Dona Speir approached me about working on her memoir, I was immediately intrigued. As she shared her background with me, I realized the depth and significance of her experiences. Her story revolved around sobriety and recovery, delving into the various addictions that plagued her life before she became a centerfold for *Playboy* magazine in the mid-1980s. What struck me the most was the redemptive aspect of her tale—how she had gone on to open homes for young women battling similar addictions.

During our conversations, there was one chilling revelation that Dona let slip. She confided in me that she had been one of the first victims of comedian Bill Cosby, who had once been considered one of America's most beloved and trusted comedians. Learning about her encounter with Cosby was a shock, and it took me a moment to process the weight of her words. Dona had never confronted this part of her story before, and was understandably apprehensive about including it in her memoir. However, I believed it was crucial to showcase the immense distance she had traveled in her life, and after careful consideration, she agreed.

Together, we worked to capture Dona's life in her memoir, which she aptly titled *The Naked Truth*. It was undoubtedly one of the most powerful endeavors I have ever worked on. Dona's story is a testament to the resilience of the human spirit and the power of personal growth. Her struggles with addiction, her path to recovery, and her subsequent efforts to establish homes for young women in need—all of it painted a clear picture of redemption.

Including her encounters with Bill Cosby was an integral part of Dona's story. It shed light on the tragic transformation of a beloved comedian into a sadistic predator. Confronting this painful chapter in her life required immense courage on Dona's part, and I was honored to be there to support her every step of the way.

As we worked on *The Naked Truth*, I became acutely aware of the immense impact this memoir could have. It had the potential to inspire and empower others facing similar challenges. Furthermore, it contributed to raising awareness about the complexities of addiction, recovery, and the devastating effects of abuse. Dona's strength and resilience were evident in every sentence we penned together.

I won't deny that the process was challenging. There were moments when Dona had to face her deepest fears head-on, reliving experiences that she had buried deep within. The process required rawness and an unwavering commitment to honesty. But with each word we penned, I could see a weight lifting off her shoulders, as if she was finally releasing the shackles that had bound her for so long. The transformative nature of writing Dona's story astounded both of us. As she confronted her own demons, she began to see the immense strength within herself. By sharing her struggles and triumphs on the page, Dona discovered that she was not alone. Others who had experienced similar pain and fear could find solace and hope in her words. It was a profound realization that her story had the power to touch lives and inspire change.

The results of writing Dona's story exceeded both of our expectations. The rewards were not only personal—they extended beyond herself. Readers reached out to share their own stories, finding comfort in the pages that mirrored their own experiences. Witnessing the result of Dona's words on others was an important reminder of the connection we all share.

Confronting the painful episodes of our lives through writing is not an easy task. It requires courage, perseverance, and a willingness to dive into the depths of our emotions. But the rewards are immeasurable. Through writing, Dona gained control, found healing, and empowered others to face their own demons.

The Naked Truth remains a powerful testament to Dona's willingness to embrace and share her past. Her memoir continues to resonate with readers, offering hope, understanding, and the knowledge that transformation is possible even in the face of unimaginable challenges.

CHAPTER 18

Frequently Asked Questions

A s a memoirist, teacher of writing workshops, and cowriter, I have encountered a variety of questions from readers, friends, and fellow writers. Some of these questions have become quite common, so I would like to share a few of them with you, along with my reflections and responses.

DOES WRITING A MEMOIR MAKE ME A NARCISSIST?

The answer to this is more nuanced than a simple "yes" or "no." While it's true that writing a memoir inherently involves focusing on oneself, it doesn't necessarily mean that the author is self-absorbed or egotistical. Memoirs are often driven by a desire to share important stories, offer insights, or provide a source of inspiration for readers. They can be deeply personal and vulnerable, serving as a means of connecting with others who may have experienced similar struggles or triumphs. In that sense, writing a memoir can be an act of empathy and generosity, rather than one of self-obsession.

Of course, like any form of writing, there can be instances where an author's ego takes center stage. Some memoirs may come across as self-indulgent or narcissistic, focusing solely on the author's achievements or the need for validation. However, it's important to recognize that this is not representative of all memoirists or the genre as a whole.

As a memoirist, my intention has always been to offer a genuine and authentic account of my life, with the aim of connecting with people on a deeper level. I believe that self-reflection and introspection are crucial for personal growth, and sharing my experiences through memoir allows me to engage in meaningful conversations with others.

Ultimately, the question of whether writing a memoir makes someone a narcissist is subjective and depends on the author's approach, intent, and the overall tone of the work. It's essential to differentiate between self-expression and self-obsession, acknowledging the potential for both within the genre.

CAN I WRITE A MEMOIR ABOUT MY PET?

Yes! Many people have written memoirs or personal narratives about their pets, sharing stories from the animal's life and their experiences together. Writing a memoir about your pet can be a wonderful way to celebrate their life and the memories you shared with them. It can also be a way to process your grief and remember the joy and love that your pet brought into your life.

When writing a memoir about your pet, you may want to consider including details about your pet's personality, habits, and favorite activities. You can also share stories about how your pet impacted your life and the lives of others around them. Including photos and other memorabilia can enhance your memoir and help bring your pet's story to life.

Writing a memoir about your pet can be a rewarding and meaningful experience, allowing you to honor the bond you shared and keep their memory alive. There are many popular memoirs written about pets. Here are some examples:

Marley & Me by John Grogan: This memoir tells the story of a Labrador retriever named Marley and his life with his family, including their adventures and misadventures together.

Dewey: The Small-Town Library Cat Who Touched the World by Vicki Myron: This memoir tells the story of a library cat named Dewey, who became a beloved fixture in his small town and affected the lives of many people.

A Cat Named Darwin by William Jordan: This memoir tells the story of a man who adopts a feral cat named Darwin, exploring their journey together as the cat learns to trust him and become a part of his family.

Homer's Odyssey by Gwen Cooper: This memoir tells the story of a blind cat named Homer and his adventures as he explores the world around him and becomes a beloved member of his family.

These memoirs are just a few examples of the many popular books written about the special relationships between people and their pets.

WHAT ARE SOME COMMON MISTAKES PEOPLE MAKE WHEN WRITING A MEMOIR?

1. **Including too much information**: Sometimes writers may include too many details or events that aren't necessary for the story. This can make the memoir feel overwhelming and difficult to follow.
2. **Focusing too much on themselves**: While memoirs are meant to focus on the author's life, it's important to remember that readers want to learn more than just what happened to the author. The author must consider how their experiences relate to larger themes or events in the world.
3. **Not having a clear narrative arc**: A memoir should have a clear beginning, middle, and end with a narrative arc that keeps readers engaged. Without a clear arc, the memoir can feel disjointed or aimless.
4. **Being too self-critical or too self-aggrandizing**: It's important to be honest about one's faults and weaknesses, but it's also important to avoid being too self-critical. Conversely, being too self-aggrandizing can come across as arrogant and unrelatable.
5. **Failing to edit and revise**: A memoir, like any other work of writing, requires careful editing and revision. Failing to edit can lead to repetition, a confusing narrative, and awkward phrasing.
6. **Not considering the impact on others**: When writing a memoir, it's important to consider how the book might affect other people who are part of the story. It's essential to be respectful and ethical when writing about others' lives and experiences.

7. **Misrepresenting facts**: Memoirs are nonfiction, and people expect them to be truthful. Avoid embellishing or changing details to make your story more interesting.

8. **Overgeneralizing**: While memoirs are personal stories, avoid making sweeping statements about groups of people or generalizing certain experiences.

9. **Focusing too much on minor details**: While well-crafted details can bring your story to life, be mindful of including too many minor details that detract from the main narrative.

10. **Using clichés**: Overused phrases and clichés can make your writing feel stale and unoriginal. Instead, strive for fresh and creative language.

11. **Writing solely for therapeutic reasons**: While writing a memoir can be therapeutic, remember that your audience is reading your book to be entertained, educated, or inspired.

12. **Ignoring the craft of storytelling**: While a memoir is a personal story, it still needs to follow the conventions of good storytelling. Ensure that your memoir has a clear structure and engages readers from beginning to end.

IS IT OKAY TO CRY WHEN PRESENTING MY STORY?

In writing workshops, I have witnessed numerous instances where a writer, overcome with emotion, finds themselves unable to hold back tears as they read their poignant and personal words aloud. It's a raw moment that can often catch both the writer and the audience off guard. Afterward, the writer may feel a sense of embarrassment or self-consciousness, unsure of how their display of emotions will be perceived.

But here's the truth that I want to share with you: those tearful moments are the most powerful and courageous ones. They signify a deep connection to the emotions and experiences being expressed through their writing. When tears flow freely, it demonstrates the writer's willingness to fully immerse themselves in their story, to feel the weight of their words, and to share their innermost truths.

These tears are not a sign of weakness or embarrassment; instead, they are a testament to the bravery and honesty of the writer. They show the writer's willingness to confront their own emotions, their past, and their readers with a level of honesty that is both courageous and transformative.

When a writer breaks down in tears while reading their work, it often evokes a powerful response in the audience as well. It creates a space of empathy and understanding, where others can witness the writer's emotions and connect on a deeply human level. It breaks down barriers and invites the audience to reflect on their own emotions and experiences.

As a teacher and facilitator, I always emphasize the importance of creating a safe and supportive environment in workshops. I encourage writers to embrace their emotions, reminding them that tears are not a sign of weakness—but rather, a sign of emotional truth. We celebrate these moments and provide a space for writers to process their emotions openly and without judgment.

So, if you find yourself moved to tears while writing or sharing your memoir, I want you to know that it is a mark of incredible strength and courage. Embrace those emotions, for they are the driving force behind your most powerful and evocative writing. Don't feel embarrassed or ashamed; recognize the transformative potential of your tears. They have the power to touch hearts, awaken empathy, and create a large impact on your readers.

Vulnerability is not a weakness—it is a superpower. Embrace it fully, honor your emotions, and let your tears become the catalyst for a truly unforgettable and life-changing piece of writing.

DO MEMOIRS HAVE TO HAVE HAPPY ENDINGS?

No, memoirs do not have to have happy endings. Memoirs are a reflection of the author's personal experiences and perspectives, and not all life experiences have a happy ending.

In fact, many memoirs explore difficult, painful, or challenging experiences, and they do not necessarily end with a neat resolution or happy ending. These memoirs may provide insight into how the author navigated through adversity, learned important lessons, or found resilience and strength in the face of hardship.

Even memoirs that explore more positive experiences may not have a traditional "happy ending." Life is often complex and messy, and memoirs can reflect that reality. A memoir may explore themes of personal growth and transformation without necessarily ending with a "happily ever after" conclusion. The ending of a memoir should reflect the author's truth and experience. As long as the memoir is authentic and honest in its portrayal of the author's journey, the ending can take on a variety of forms, both positive and negative.

HOW IMPORTANT IS RESEARCH IN MEMOIR WRITING?

Research is incredibly important when crafting a memoir; in fact, I cannot emphasize its significance enough. As I delve into the process of shaping my personal narrative, research serves as the backbone and the foundation upon which my memoir is built.

Research adds depth and credibility to my storytelling. Although my memoir is rooted in my own experiences and memories, incorporating well-researched facts, historical context, and cultural references enriches the narrative and provides a broader perspective. Through diligent research, I can enhance the authenticity and accuracy of my memoir, ensuring that it connects with readers and offers a more comprehensive understanding of the events, people, and societal dynamics that shaped my story.

Additionally, research helps me fill in gaps in my memory. Memories, especially those from distant years, can be hazy or incomplete. Engaging in thorough research allows me to reconstruct the past more accurately, refreshing my recollections and providing a more nuanced portrayal of the events I am recounting. By exploring relevant archives, documents, photographs, and even conducting interviews with individuals who were part of my story, I can gain new insights and uncover forgotten details that contribute to a more memorable and comprehensive memoir.

Research helps me gain a broader perspective on my own experiences. It enables me to place my personal narrative within a larger historical, cultural, or social context. By understanding the broader forces and events that were at play during specific periods of my life, I can better articulate the importance they had on me and my story. Research allows me to explore the societal, political, or cultural climate of the time, shedding light on the motivations, challenges, and choices that shaped my story. This perspective not only enriches my memoir but provides readers with valuable insights into the world in which my story unfolds.

Research also offers me the opportunity to learn from other memoirists and writers who have tackled similar themes or experiences. By studying their works, I can gain inspiration, gather stylistic techniques, and deepen my understanding of the craft. This engagement with the literary world allows me to refine my own storytelling skills, enhance the structure and narrative arc of my memoir, and find my unique voice amidst a rich tapestry of literary voices.

Lastly, research helps maintain ethical integrity in my memoir. It ensures that I respect the privacy and dignity of individuals mentioned in my story, especially when recounting real-life encounters or interactions. By researching facts, cross-referencing events, and seeking multiple perspectives, I can present a balanced and fair account of my experiences, avoiding misunderstandings or misrepresentations that may inadvertently occur when relying solely on memory.

WHAT CAN YOU TELL ME ABOUT COLLABORATING WITH OTHERS?

This book's primary purpose is to guide you in writing your own story. However, there may come a time when you find yourself collaborating with someone else and helping them bring their own story to life. It's during these moments that questions arise about the collaborative process and how to create an environment that fosters open sharing, enabling the creation of an effective narrative. With the multitude of people I've had the privilege to write with, I often find myself being asked about this very process. So, let me share my thoughts and experiences with you.

First and foremost, creating a safe and supportive environment is essential for collaborative writing. Trust is the foundation upon which meaningful collaborations are built. Show empathy, respect, and genuine care for the person you're working with. Listen actively and create space for them to express themselves without judgment. Make it clear that their story matters, and that you are there to support them every step of the way.

Communication is key. Establish open lines of dialogue from the beginning. Encourage honest conversation about their goals, fears, and expectations for the project. Regularly check in, seeking feedback and addressing any concerns that may arise. A collaborative writing process requires active participation from both parties, so ensure that your intentions and visions align.

Flexibility is also crucial. Recognize that each person's writing path is unique, and some may need time to reflect and process before opening up. Others may prefer a more structured approach. Adapt your methods and techniques to suit their needs. Be patient and understand that it takes time to cultivate vulnerability.

Above all, be a compassionate listener. Allow your collaborator to share their experiences at their own pace. Be present and attentive, understanding that their story is deeply personal and may bring forth a range of emotions. Show empathy and provide a safe space for them to explore their narrative fully.

Remember, the goal is to create an effective story. Help your collaborator uncover the core themes, motivations, and emotions that drive their narrative. Offer guidance and support in crafting a compelling structure and solid prose. Collaborate on editing and revising, always with the intention of enhancing the story's power.

Collaborative writing is an opportunity to help someone else share their unique experiences with the world. By fostering a nurturing environment, cultivating trust, and maintaining open lines of communication, you can play a vital role in shaping a story that captivates readers.

Writing a memoir in someone else's voice involves a great deal of empathy and imagination on the part of you, the writer. To accurately capture and convey the voice of another person, you must first immerse yourself in that person's experiences, emotions, and thoughts, as well as their individual mannerisms, speech patterns, and idiosyncrasies.

To channel someone else's energy onto the page, you must be able to think and feel as that person would. This requires a deep understanding of the person's personality, motivations, and beliefs, as well as their unique perspective on the world.

You must also be attentive to the nuances of the person's language and tone, and strive to capture these elements in their writing. This may involve listening to recordings of the person speaking, reading their personal writings or correspondence, and conducting interviews with them or others who know them well.

In the end, the goal is to create a narrative that feels authentic and true to the person's experience and voice. You, the writer, must be willing to let go of your own voice and ego, and allow the voice of the other person to come through in the writing. This requires a great deal of skill, sensitivity, and creativity. It is a challenging but rewarding process for any writer to take on the task of writing a memoir in someone else's voice.

CAN A COMPANY OR BRAND HAVE A MEMOIR?

Yes, there is such a thing as a corporate memoir. A corporate memoir is a type of book or written document that tells the story of a company, its history, and its impact on the industry or community. Corporate memoirs can be written by the company's founders, executives, or outside authors who have been given access to the company's archives and leadership.

Corporate memoirs can serve several purposes, such as providing inspiration and motivation to employees, establishing a company's brand identity, preserving its legacy, and educating customers and investors about the company's history and values. Corporate memoirs can also be used as a marketing tool to build a company's reputation and credibility.

While corporate memoirs can be valuable resources for employees, customers, and investors, it's essential to ensure that the memoir is accurate and doesn't present a biased or overly positive view of the company's history. It's also important to ensure that confidential or proprietary information is not disclosed in the memoir.

Corporate memoirs can provide valuable insights into the inner workings of companies, their successes, and their failures. Here are some examples of corporate memoirs:

Shoe Dog by Phil Knight: The memoir of Nike's founder, Phil Knight, which takes us through the early days of Nike's formation and the company's growth into a global brand.

Pour Your Heart Into It by Howard Schultz: The memoir of Howard Schultz, the CEO of Starbucks, which details the company's rise to success and the challenges faced along the way.

Losing My Virginity by Richard Branson: The memoir of Richard Branson, the founder of Virgin Group, which provides a candid account of his entrepreneurial journey from the founding of his first business to the growth of the Virgin empire.

The Hard Thing About Hard Things by Ben Horowitz: The memoir of Ben Horowitz, a venture capitalist and cofounder of the software company LoudCloud, provides practical advice for entrepreneurs facing difficult challenges in the world of startups.

Grinding It Out by Ray Kroc: The memoir of Ray Kroc, the man who turned McDonald's into a global fast-food empire, provides insights into Kroc's business philosophy and the challenges he faced in building the McDonald's brand.

These memoirs offer valuable insights into the minds of successful business leaders and can provide inspiration for aspiring entrepreneurs.

HOW LONG SHOULD MY MEMOIR BE?

There is no set length for a memoir, as it can vary based on the author's preference and the story they want to tell. Generally, memoirs range from around 50,000 to 100,000 words, but some may be longer or shorter depending on the subject matter and the writing style. Ultimately, the length of the memoir should be determined by however many words the author needs to tell their story effectively and engagingly.

DO I NEED PERMISSION TO WRITE ABOUT OTHERS?

Legally, you are not required to get permission before writing about others in your memoir. However, it is a good ethical practice to consider how your portrayal of them may affect their privacy and reputation. If you plan to publish your memoir, it's important to be mindful of how your words may affect others, especially if you plan to include personal and potentially sensitive information about individuals who are still alive.

I recommend informing people who may be mentioned in your memoir that you are writing it and giving them an opportunity to share their thoughts and concerns about being included. Some people may be comfortable with you writing about them, while others may not want to be featured in your memoir. If someone expresses concerns about being included, consider adjusting your writing accordingly.

SHOULD I WORK WITH A WRITING COACH?

Working with a writing coach can be a good idea when writing a memoir, as a coach can provide personalized guidance and support throughout the writing process. Here are some potential benefits of working with a writing coach when writing a memoir:

Expert guidance: A writing coach can provide expert guidance on the writing process, helping you to develop a clear structure and strategy for your memoir, and providing feedback on your writing style and technique.

Accountability: A writing coach can help keep you accountable for your writing goals, providing regular check-ins and deadlines to ensure that you make steady progress toward completing your memoir.

Emotional support: Writing a memoir can be a deeply personal and emotional process, and a writing coach can provide emotional support and encouragement.

Problem-solving: A writing coach can help you navigate any challenges or obstacles that may arise during the writing process—such as writer's block, self-doubt, or creative roadblocks.

Perspective: A writing coach can provide an objective perspective on your writing, offering insights and suggestions that can help you to refine and improve your memoir.

Working with a writing coach can be a valuable investment for memoir writers who want to receive personalized guidance and support throughout the writing process.

WHAT ABOUT WRITER'S BLOCK?

Writer's block is a common phenomenon that occurs when a writer has difficulty generating new ideas or making progress on a writing project. It can manifest as a feeling of being stuck or unable to move forward, and it can be a frustrating and discouraging experience. There are many possible causes of writer's block, including fear of failure, perfectionism, lack of inspiration, and burnout. However, there are several strategies that writers can use to overcome writer's block and get back to writing:

Freewriting: Freewriting involves setting a timer for a set amount of time and writing continuously without worrying about grammar, spelling, or punctuation. The goal is to generate as many ideas as possible without worrying about if they are good.

Brainstorming: Brainstorming involves generating a list of ideas related to a particular topic or theme. This can help spark new ideas and get the creative juices flowing.

Changing your environment: Sometimes a change of scenery can help to break through writer's block. Try writing in a different location, such as a coffee shop, library, or park.

Taking breaks: Taking a break from writing and engaging in other activities, such as exercise or meditation, can help to clear the mind and reduce stress.

Setting small goals: Setting small, achievable goals can help build momentum and create a sense of accomplishment. For example, setting a goal of writing for ten minutes each day can help establish a regular writing practice.

Writer's block is a normal part of the writing process. Thankfully, it's possible to overcome it with patience, persistence, and a willingness to try new strategies. Writing can be a demanding and stressful activity, so it's important for you, as a writer, to take breaks and engage in activities that promote relaxation and well-being. Here are some suggestions for how writers can relax:

Take a walk: Going for a walk can help to clear the mind, reduce stress, and boost creativity. Taking a break from writing to get some fresh air and exercise can refresh and rejuvenate the mind and body.

Practice mindfulness: Mindfulness practices—such as meditation, deep breathing, or yoga—can help reduce stress and increase focus and clarity. Taking a few minutes to engage in mindfulness practices can help writers feel more centered and relaxed.

Listen to music: Listening to music can be a powerful mood booster and stress reliever. Whether it's classical, jazz, or your favorite pop songs, listening to music can reduce stress and enhance creativity.

Engage in a hobby: Taking part in a hobby—such as gardening, cooking, or painting—can help writers take a break from writing and engage in a different activity. Pursuing a hobby can help you relax and increase overall well-being.

Spend time with loved ones: Spending time with family and friends can be a great way to relax and recharge. Social connections can help promote happiness and well-being.

Take a break: Whether it's for a few hours or a few days, taking time away from writing can help writers recharge and come back to their work with fresh energy and perspective.

It's important for you to find ways to relax and recharge in order to maintain your creativity and well-being.

There's one other take on writer's block I'd like to share. Even though it can feel like an insurmountable obstacle, what if we were to shift our perspective and see writer's block not as a hindrance, but as a gentle nudge from the universe? Perhaps it is our body and mind's way of signaling to us that it's time to pause, to take a step back, and to breathe.

Writer's block, far from being a foe to be feared, can be a friendly reminder that rest and rejuvenation are essential parts of the creative process. It is a signal that our well of inspiration may be running low, and that it's time to replenish it. In these moments of apparent stagnation, we have an opportunity to embrace stillness, to immerse ourselves in the world around us, and to engage in activities that nourish our spirits.

Rather than viewing writer's block as a roadblock on our creative journey, we can choose to see it as a detour leading us towards self-care and renewal. It is an invitation to step away from the page, to explore new experiences, and to allow our minds to wander freely. By embracing these moments of pause, we open ourselves up to the possibility of new insights and fresh perspectives.

So, the next time writer's block pays you a visit, remember that it is not something to be scared of or worried about. Instead, perhaps see it as a gentle prompting to take a break, to recharge, and to regenerate. Trust that this period of rest is an essential part of the creative process, one that will ultimately lead you back to the page with a renewed sense of energy and purpose.

DOES AI AFFECT MEMOIR WRITING?

While artificial intelligence (AI) and technology can offer various tools and aids to assist writers, they cannot replace the essence of writing itself. Writing is a deeply personal and creative endeavor that involves self-expression and reflection.

AI can provide grammar and spelling suggestions, help with research, or generate ideas based on patterns and data analysis. It can even generate text based on prompts or existing content. These capabilities can be valuable in terms of efficiency and inspiration, especially for those who struggle with certain aspects of writing. However, AI lacks the human touch, emotion, and unique voice that make writing truly compelling.

The process of writing involves more than just the end result. It encompasses the exploration of ideas, as well as the ability to convey thoughts and emotions authentically. Writing allows us to connect with ourselves and others on a deeper level. It is a means of self-expression and a path to understanding.

It's important for writers to embrace technology as a tool but not rely on it entirely. Writing is a craft that requires practice, dedication, and personal effort. It's about finding your voice, developing your style, and embracing the challenges and joys that come with it.

So, while AI can offer assistance and convenience, the decision to truly write and experience the process remains in the hands of the writer. It's a choice to sit down, pour your thoughts onto the page, and let your words flow. That decision cannot be replaced or fulfilled by technology alone.

I often recall Ernest Hemingway's words: "There is nothing to writing. All you do is sit down at a typewriter and bleed." This quote comes to mind whenever this topic comes up. I view it this way: if I were to rely on a machine, like an AI, to help me with my first-person narrative, I would be robbing myself of what Hemingway referred to as the "bleeding" process. In other words, the raw and visceral act of putting pen to paper or fingers to keyboard is just as important as the final product itself. That's another reason why I never worry about the encroachment of technology, like computers, on first-person narrative writing. If I am truly driven to write my memoir, then the act of writing it becomes as significant as the finished work. It's about embracing the process, immersing myself in the emotions and experiences, and letting the words flow from within.

CHAPTER 19

Making a Schedule

A s you know by now, writing a memoir is a personal and unique process. As a result, the timeline can vary depending on individual circumstances. However, I still wanted to provide you with general outlines for a schedule to write your memoir. Keep in mind that these schedules can be adjusted based on your writing speed, availability, and personal preferences.

SIX-MONTH SCHEDULE TO WRITE YOUR PERSONAL MEMOIR:

Month 1: Preparation and Reflection

1. Reflect on your life experiences and identify the key themes and stories you want to include in your memoir.
2. Create a detailed outline or a chapter-by-chapter breakdown of your memoir.
3. Set specific writing goals for each month and establish a writing routine.

Month 2–3: Researching and Gathering Materials

1. Conduct any necessary research to supplement your memories and provide context.
2. Collect photographs, letters, journals, and any other relevant materials that can enhance your memoir.
3. Organize your research materials and incorporate them into your outline.

Month 4–5: Writing and Drafting

1. Begin writing the first draft of your memoir, starting with the chapters that come most easily to you.
2. Focus on capturing the essence of your experiences and emotions rather than perfecting the writing.
3. Aim to write consistently, setting aside dedicated time each day or week to work on your memoir.

Month 6: Editing and Revisions

1. Take a break from writing and let your first draft sit for a while.
2. Start the editing process by reviewing your draft for clarity, coherence, and structure.
3. Revise and polish your memoir, paying attention to language, pacing, and storytelling techniques.
4. Seek feedback from trusted friends, family, or writing groups, and incorporate their suggestions.
5. Consider hiring a professional editor to provide additional feedback and help refine your memoir.

By following this six-month schedule, you can make significant progress in writing your memoir. Remember to be flexible and adapt the timeline to suit your needs and circumstances. Good luck with your writing!

TWELVE-MONTH SCHEDULE TO WRITE YOUR PERSONAL MEMOIR:

Month 1: Preparation and Reflection

1. Reflect on your life experiences and determine the central theme or focus of your memoir.
2. Outline the major events and stories you want to include.
3. Establish your motivation and goals for writing your memoir.

Month 2–3: Researching and Gathering Materials

1. Conduct any necessary research to supplement your memories and provide context.
2. Collect photographs, letters, journals, or any other relevant materials that can enhance your memoir.
3. Organize your research materials and incorporate them into your outline.

Month 4–5: Writing and Drafting

1. Begin writing the first draft of your memoir, starting with the chapters that come most naturally to you.
2. Set a regular writing schedule and commit to writing consistently.
3. Focus on capturing the essence of your experiences, emotions, and unique voice.

Month 6–7: Review and Revisions (Part 1)

1. Take a break from writing and let your first draft sit for a while.
2. Review the draft with a fresh perspective, focusing on overall structure, pacing, and coherence.
3. Make necessary revisions and edits to improve the flow and clarity of your memoir.

Month 8–9: Review and Revisions (Part 2)

1. Dive deeper into the content of your memoir, focusing on individual chapters and sections.
2. Refine the language, imagery, and storytelling techniques to enhance the reader's experience.
3. Consider seeking feedback from beta readers or a writing group to gain different perspectives.

Month 10–11: Final Editing and Proofreading

1. Conduct a thorough line-by-line editing pass to eliminate grammar, spelling, and punctuation errors.
2. Pay attention to consistency in tone, style, and voice throughout your memoir.
3. Consider hiring a professional editor to provide a comprehensive edit and feedback on your work.

Month 12: Publication and Promotion

1. Decide on the publishing route—traditional publishing or self-publishing—if interested.
2. If traditional publishing, start pitching publishers and/or agents. If self-publishing, format your manuscript for publication as an eBook or print book.
3. Develop a marketing and promotional plan to generate awareness and interest in your memoir.
4. Celebrate!

CHAPTER 20

In Closing

So, we made it. Well done!

You now have the tools to identify which parts of your life you want to write about. You've discovered the art of storytelling and how to effectively convey your experiences. Understanding the importance of "show, don't tell" and utilizing your senses to create vivid descriptions has become second nature to you. And hey, you're even getting the hang of writing meaningful dialogue!

You've learned the value of outlining and structuring your memoir, which gives your writing a solid foundation. Choosing meaningful themes to drive your story has become a priority. Establishing a writing routine, one that works for you, will prove to be a game changer—I promise. By setting up a schedule, you're staying focused and disciplined, making steady progress on your writing.

Let's not forget the power of keeping a journal, as it's an invaluable tool for capturing your thoughts and experiences. You've also discovered the significance of reading your stories aloud, aiming to refine your work and ensure it resonates with your readers.

As you continue on this path, you'll gain insights into approaching agents and publishers. This step will be crucial in sharing your work with a broader audience, and I have no doubt you'll navigate it with confidence and success.

I genuinely wish you the very best, and who knows—maybe one day, you'll have the opportunity to join one of my workshops. Connecting with fellow writers in that way is truly inspiring. But for now, I hope you find this book helpful as you continue to follow your personal writing experience.

THE MEMOIRIST CREDO

The memoirist credo is a set of principles I have created that guides writers working in the memoir genre. While there is no one-size-fits-all credo that applies to every memoirist, there are a few common themes and beliefs that I believe many writers in this genre share.

First and foremost, the memoirist credo emphasizes the importance of honesty and authenticity. Memoirists believe it is essential to tell the truth—even if it's difficult or uncomfortable—and to present a clear and accurate representation of their experiences and emotions.

In addition to honesty, memoirists value introspection and self-reflection. They believe it's important to examine their own thoughts and feelings, to explore the reasons behind their actions, and to gain a deeper understanding of themselves and their place in the world.

Memoirists also often place a high value on the craft of writing itself. They believe that memoirs should be well-written, with careful attention paid to language, structure, and pacing. They strive to create narratives that are compelling and emotionally resonant, using their skills as writers to bring their stories to life on the page.

Remember, immersing yourself in the craft of writing is crucial to your growth as a writer. Embrace the opportunity to learn from established authors, engage in discussions with fellow students or writers, and actively seek out new reading material. By continuously expanding your knowledge, practicing your skills, and connecting with others in the writing community, you will develop a strong foundation as a writer and embark on a fulfilling creative journey.

Finally, the memoirist credo emphasizes the importance of empathy and compassion. Memoirists believe that, by sharing their own stories, they can help others feel less alone, gain new insights into their own experiences, and connect with others on a deeper level. They see the act of writing as a powerful tool for building bridges between people of different backgrounds and experiences, and they strive to use their writing to create a more compassionate and understanding world.

Let's not forget where we began our journey together—with the John Cheever quote that inspired this book's title: "A good page of prose is where one hears the rain." When I come across a well-written page of prose, it has the remarkable ability to transport me to another world. It pulls me in so deeply that I feel as though I'm right there, experiencing the story unfold. The rain mentioned by John Cheever becomes more than just words on a page; it becomes a sensory experience that surrounds me, making the story come alive.

For me, a good page of prose goes beyond mere immersion. It serves as a reminder that I am not alone in this world. It lets me know that there are others out there giving voice to something I may believe in, learn from, or feel deeply affected by. It's a comforting feeling, knowing that someone has captured the essence of my thoughts, emotions, or struggles and has expressed them in such a profound and relatable way.

In those moments, literature becomes a powerful connector. It bridges the gap between individuals, transcending time, space, and personal circumstances. It reminds me that there are others who have experienced similar joys, pains, doubts, and hopes. It makes me feel like part of a larger community where my thoughts and feelings are shared and understood.

Beyond the sense of belonging, a good page of prose also has the potential to offer insights, knowledge, and wisdom. It opens up new perspectives, challenges my assumptions, and expands my understanding of the world. Through literature, I can learn about different cultures, historical events, scientific discoveries, and philosophical concepts. It's an enriching experience that broadens my horizons and encourages personal growth.

In this way, a good page of prose becomes more than just entertainment or escape. It becomes a profound connection to the human experience. It reminds me that I am not alone in my journey through life, and it offers me the opportunity to explore, learn, and evolve. It gives voice to something greater than myself and leaves a lasting impact, shaping my thoughts, emotions, and beliefs long after I've turned the page.

I remember a stormy summer day when I found myself at John Cheever's house. The darkness outside seemed to permeate the atmosphere inside his office. Something was clearly troubling him, as our usual sessions of discussing my stories and making notes seemed distant. He hardly said anything that day.

I settled into my chair while he remained behind his desk, staring pensively at the woods through the rain-streaked window.

The thunder cracked and the heavy raindrops splattered against the warm flagstone outside. He appeared tired, perhaps even a bit frustrated. But despite his silence, his words during that moment have stayed with me ever since. He finally broke the silence and spoke directly to me, his voice carrying a weight of wisdom and experience.

"Remember, if you say you're going to write, then write. Keep doing what you're doing. As you get older, you'll encounter countless people who talk about writing, who describe the books they feel they have in them and dream of penning. But the one thing they won't ever do is write. Don't be like that. If you truly want to be a writer, then never stop writing. Write every day."

His words hit me hard, cutting through the doubts and insecurities that often plague aspiring writers. There was an urgency in his voice, a sense that he had learned this lesson through years of dedication and discipline. It was a reminder that writing isn't just about dreaming or talking about it—it's about the act of putting pen to paper or fingers to keyboard, consistently, persistently.

That day, in that dimly lit office, I realized that writing is a commitment—a commitment to myself, to the stories within me, and to the craft itself. It's about showing up every day, even when inspiration is elusive or the world seems to conspire against it. It's about embracing the process, the highs and lows, the frustrations and breakthroughs.

John Cheever's words continue to echo in my mind, guiding me through the challenges and doubts that come with being a writer. They serve as a constant reminder that if I want to fulfill my aspirations, I must remain dedicated, disciplined, and unwavering in my pursuit. So, whenever I find myself faltering or questioning my path, I hear his voice urging me to keep writing, to keep creating, to never lose sight of the passion that drives me. That stormy day at John Cheever's house became a pivotal moment in my writing journey. It was a moment of clarity and motivation, a moment that instilled in me the resolve to keep writing—no matter what. And for that, I'll forever be grateful.

If you've read this book, it's because you *have* to write. So I encourage you, go write. Think about your story. Think about what you bring to the world. Think about how you can change somebody's life by sharing something that you have gone through. Everybody has something worth sharing. Everybody has truth worth confronting. Everybody has fears worth facing.

Writing a memoir is a wonderful way to accomplish all of those things—and many more—but success doesn't have to be in the form of a book. It can be a story once in a while. It can be some precious anecdote you've been dying to get off your chest. Don't get hamstrung with the idea that you have to go write a book. You may want to, and that's great. But if being an author is not what interests you, that's fine. Being a writer is far more important.

So go find your stories. Go find your truths. Go find those universal experiences that we can all learn and grow from.

One last Cheever memory: It was June 1982, just after I had wrapped up my junior year at Emerson College in Boston. I had been aware that Mr. Cheever had been battling cancer and his health had been deteriorating. There were moments when

I would call him, and I could hear the weakness and raspiness in his voice. I had wanted to interview him for an article I was working on for a local publication, but it became evident that he was too frail for such an undertaking.

However, despite his declining health, Cheever had shown me great kindness. Earlier that year, he had reached out to a professor in Boston on my behalf, putting in a good word for me. I was incredibly grateful because it helped me secure a spot in a writers' salon organized by some of the professors.

Looking back, I realize that I may not have fully appreciated the significance of the mentorship relationship I had with John Cheever. At the time, a part of me pursued it to please my father, who held John in high regard and adored his work. It was less about me and more about my father, whom I was not close with (yet I yearned and even dreamed of a closer relationship with him).

When I learned of John Cheever's passing on the news, I was filled with sadness. It was a poignant reminder of the impact he had on my life, and I couldn't help but feel a pang of regret. It was a missed opportunity to not have fully recognized and cherished, in the moment, the mentorship I had received from such a talented and respected writer.

Reflecting upon those memories, I now obviously realize the profound influence he had on my life. I am grateful for the support Mr. Cheever provided, and I wish I had expressed my appreciation more openly while he was still with us. I recognize how incredibly fortunate I was to have had the opportunity to be in the presence of such greatness. However, during those years, I was just a teenager with my interests scattered in a million different directions. From tennis to girls, from my friends to my family, my attention was pulled in various directions. Sometimes, meeting with John Cheever felt like a chore—discussing my stories, deciphering his notes, and navigating the writing process.

I am grateful for the time I spent in the company of John Cheever, even if my teenage self didn't fully grasp the magnitude of the experience. His words continue to inspire and influence me, serving as a constant reminder of the power and beauty of storytelling.

It is my sincere hope that readers like yourself will find solace, inspiration, and a connection with these recollections. This book is a tribute to John Cheever, a celebration of his remarkable talent, and a humble acknowledgment of the influence he had on shaping the course of my life.

Thank you so much for being part of this experience with me.

P.S. Go start writing. Now.

AFTERWORD

When I originally came to Chris for help with my memoir, I was coming off what you could best characterize as a "really bad writing relationship." I was forced to have a cowriter who did not do the work and just wanted to record sound bites of me on TV shows, which had nothing to do with what my memoir, *Just Tyrus*, was about. I was trying to tell my story in my words, and I was completely open about the fact that I had to learn how to be a writer. It was something that I wasn't sure I could do, but I wanted to give it a try.

In meeting with Chris, he listened to me. That was the first thing. He's a great listener. He doesn't interrupt. And when I say that, it means when you're telling your story, he doesn't try to mold it. He basically lets you see your words as "clay," and he sees that you're trying to make a vase. He waits until the vase turns over sideways and spills all over the floor, and then he's like, "Okay, look what we've got. This is where we're going to start from, right here." And then he helps you mold it. All you'll see is an ugly ass vase, but then you have the ability to mold it and control it. And then, after we discuss something, the teaching begins.

I don't like saying Chris is simply a writing teacher. He does more than that. He's teaching you how to work your feelings and your emotions into something that is palatable for other people. And at the same time, you're learning something. The longer you spend with Chris, the more comfortable you are with opening up about stuff.

They say musical geniuses can supposedly "see" the notes in the air. Chris makes you see the words as they come out of your mouth. That's the best way I can describe it. He made me see the words when I was learning and working on my book, and it became easier. It's still a lot of hard work. It's a lot of hours. But you understand the writing process with him. He guides you like a craftsman. I think of Chris as Geppetto because he makes things real. He wants everything that's special in you to come out.

So keep this book handy, even after you finish reading it. Like he says, your story is never really finished. This book is like having Chris right by your side, shaping that clay, while also carving you into the best writer and storyteller you can be.

— **Tyrus,** former pro wrestler, popular network news commentator, and bestselling author

FURTHER READING

Here are some highly recommended books about how to write memoir:

The Memoir Project: A Thoroughly Non-Standardized Text for Writing & Life by Marion Roach Smith — This book offers practical advice on how to write a memoir, including tips on how to structure your story, find your voice, and handle sensitive topics.

Bird by Bird: Some Instructions on Writing and Life by Anne Lamott — Through personal anecdotes and practical tips, Lamott provides readers with a compassionate and down-to-earth perspective on the challenges and joys of writing.

Writing Life Stories: How to Make Memories into Memoirs, Ideas into Essays, and Life into Literature by Bill Roorbach — This book covers the basics of memoir writing, from choosing a topic to organizing your material and creating a compelling narrative.

The Art of Memoir by Mary Karr — This book combines writing advice with personal anecdotes from the author's own life, offering insights on how to write with honesty and emotional depth.

Old Friend from Far Away: The Practice of Writing Memoir by Natalie Goldberg — This book provides a series of writing prompts and exercises designed to help writers explore their memories and turn them into powerful memoirs.

Handling the Truth: On the Writing of Memoir by Beth Kephart — This book offers practical advice on how to write memoir, including tips on how to handle difficult material, create a strong voice, and build a compelling narrative.

On Writing: A Memoir of the Craft by Stephen King — Although not specifically a book on memoir writing, this book offers invaluable insights on the craft of writing, including advice on how to craft unforgettable characters and create a sense of urgency and suspense in your writing.

The Situation and the Story: The Art of Personal Narrative by Vivian Gornick — This book explores the relationship between the "situation" (the events of a memoir) and the "story" (the narrative structure and theme), offering guidance on how to balance both elements effectively.

The Elements of Style by William Strunk Jr. and E. B. White — This is a classic guide to writing that has been used by generations of writers and students to improve their writing skills. The book was originally published in 1918 by

Strunk Jr., a professor of English at Cornell University, and was later revised and updated by White, a renowned writer and essayist. The book offers practical advice and rules for writing clear, concise, and effective prose. It covers topics such as grammar, punctuation, usage, and style, and it provides examples and exercises to help writers master these elements. *The Elements of Style* emphasizes the importance of clarity and simplicity in writing. It encourages writers to avoid unnecessary words and phrases, to use active voice instead of passive voice, and to strive for precision and accuracy in their writing. These principles have become widely accepted as standards for good writing and are still taught in many writing programs today.

WRITING PROMPTS

I'm not quite done with you yet.... Here are some parting prompts to keep you busy for a while.

1. Write about a turning point in your life. What happened, and how did it change you?
2. Write about a difficult decision you had to make. What factors did you consider, and how did you ultimately decide what to do?
3. Write about a significant event or moment in your childhood. What memories stand out, and how did they shape who you are today?
4. Write about a place that holds special meaning for you. What memories do you associate with that place, and why is it important to you?
5. Write about a person who has had a profound impact on your life. How did you meet, and what did they teach you?
6. Write about a mistake you made and what you learned from it. How did it change your life, and how did you move forward?

7. Write about a challenge you faced and overcame. What strategies did you use, and how did you grow as a result?

8. Write about a dream or goal you had and achieved. How did you work toward it, and how did it feel to finally accomplish it?

9. Write about a relationship that was important to you. What did you learn from it, and how did it shape your life?

10. Write about a moment of clarity or a realization you had. What did you discover, and how did it change your perspective?

11. "Snapshot": Choose a photograph from your past and write a scene based on the image. Focus on sensory details and emotions to bring the scene to life.

12. "People Watching": Sit in a public place and observe the people around you. Choose one person and imagine their life story, writing a short piece about them.

13. "Music Memories": Choose a song that has special meaning to you and write a memoir piece about the memories and emotions associated with it.

14. "Childhood Memories": Think back to your childhood and write a memoir piece about a memory from that time. Focus on sensory details and emotions to bring the memory to life.

15. "Travelogue": Choose a place you have traveled to and write a memoir piece about your experiences there. Focus on the sensory details and emotions associated with the place.

ACKNOWLEDGMENTS

I would like to thank Anthony Ziccardi and Jacob Hoye at Post Hill Press for their faith in this project. Thank you to my editor, Rachel Hoge, as well. Huge thank yous to John Oates and Tyrus for their contributions. Special thanks to the Friends of the Library at the Newport Beach Public Library for their generous support of my writing workshops. Additionally, big thanks to Programs Specialist, Terry Sanchez, and Library Service Manager, Rebecca Lightfoot, also at the Newport Public Library. Special thanks to all of my writing students over the years, most notably Judee Schultz, William Hall, Margot Wagner, Armida Gordon, Anna Christine Linder-Skach, Christine O'Connor, Darvy Cohan, Albert LoSchiavo, SuAnne White, Robert O'Brien, Barbara Hunt, Cassie Thomas, Lorena Ortega, Dolores Curry, Jimmy Torrejon, and Elisabeth Gegner. Last but not least, to my children, Charles and Claire, two fine writers themselves and forever the two brightest lights in my life.

ABOUT THE AUTHOR

Memoirist Chris Epting has a distinguished career that spans over a dozen popular memoirs, including collaborations with notable figures such as John Oates, the Doobie Brothers, Leif Garrett, Tyrus, Dave Mason, Olympian Shirley Babashoff, Def Leppard's Phil Collen, and others. Epting brings a wealth of experience and wisdom to aspiring writers. Also, as an award-winning journalist and author of many popular nonfiction titles from travel to sports to pop culture, Epting's storytelling skills have made him a popular guest on many television and radio programs.